STRONG IN SPIRIT

5-MINUTE DEVOTIONS FOR PRETEEN BOYS

David S. Winston

Niki Winston

Illustrations by TheLittleLabs Studio

CALLISTO PUBLISHING

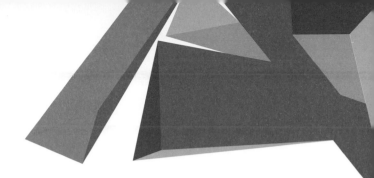

We dedicate this book to our four

children, Jacob, Jordan, Lily, and Joshua.

Thank you, Joshua, for all of your time

and input into each of these devotions.

Because of your insight, your forever

imprint is on this book, and you've had

a hand in the spiritual growth of

many young men like yourself.

We love you all so very much!

Mom & Dad

INTRODUCTION

Welcome to *Strong in Spirit*! We are excited and grateful to begin this journey with you. Right now, you are either in middle school or headed that way pretty soon. As a preteen boy, you've got a lot going on. School, friends, parents, and siblings can give a kid a lot to think about, not to mention things you're reading and seeing on TV and in the media (and even random thoughts that come into your head). And before you know it, you'll be in high school and have to make more grown-up decisions—a thought that might sound exciting, scary, or a combination of both. This book will help you get the spiritual foundation you need as you continue to grow and learn. The lessons you learn here will provide guidance for the challenges you face every day and will teach you how to confidently approach any decisions you have to make, now or in the future.

Having both grown up in Christian households, we (Pastor David and Niki) know what it's like to be a young Christian and love God but also sometimes be confused about how to please Him. That's why we decided to write this book—we wish we had a guide like this back then, so that we could have more easily understood how God feels about the things preteens face every day. Though some things about being a preteen are timeless, a lot of other things have changed since we were young—so our (now) 11-year-old son Joshua helped us make sure this book's content was current and relevant and answered the kinds of questions kids have right now.

Strong in Spirit is organized into one devotion per page. You can read each devotion in about five minutes, so it's easy to read one every day. You might want to read in the morning, right when you wake up, or, if you like to read before bed, in the evening, right before you go to sleep. You can read the book straight through from beginning to end, or flip through the pages and find a topic that speaks to whatever you're feeling that day. We talk about everything from faith and wisdom to crushes and bullying.

At the end of each devotion is a prompt to inspire reflection. This is designed to help you think a bit more about the devotion you just read. It might ask you to answer questions, write about something, or plan things you can do in the future to put what you just learned into action. Some devotions also include prayers that help you understand more about that day's lesson.

Some of these devotions may leave you with questions or concerns. Any time you have questions or want to talk about something you've read, be sure to go to your parent or guardian or another trusted adult. They won't just answer your questions— they'll appreciate the opportunity to have a great discussion as well. You might even want to read your devotions with a family member each day, for some extra quality time together.

As you grow, you're probably having a lot of new thoughts and feelings and encountering a lot of new information. It's great to learn new things! But sometimes, it's hard to know which information is good and which is bad, what's true and what's false. You need to have good information in order to make good decisions—if you have bad information, like Adam and Eve had when the devil lied to them, you make bad decisions. God's Word is good information, and following it will always lead you to good decisions. That's why we wrote this book—to give you the truth from God's Word, so you can grow closer to God, become stronger in your faith, and always know the right thing to do. As you read, we pray you will receive God's wisdom to know what's right and the courage to help you make the right decisions.

WHAT IS FAITH?

Now faith is confidence in what we hope for and assurance
about what we do not see . . . By faith we understand that
the universe was formed at God's command, so that
what is seen was not made out of what was visible.

HEBREWS 11:1, 3

You know your bed is real. You can see it, you can touch it, you can
even lie on it. Because you can see your bed, you "believe in it," and
no one can convince you that it doesn't exist. But God asks us to
believe in what we cannot see. This is called faith.

We can see the world around us, full of God's creations—people,
plants and trees, animals, the sky. But they didn't just appear. They
were created by God, just like you and I were created by Him. We
can believe that the created things exist because we see them, but
we must also be able to believe in things we can't see (like love and
truth). God created the universe and everything in it, so since we
can put our faith in the creation, we should put much more of our
faith in the *Creator*.

We also put our faith in God's Word and what it says. It says that
Jesus died on the cross for our sins and rose again on the third day.
We didn't see Him do this, but by faith, we believe with our whole
hearts that He did it. We have new life and forgiveness of sins
because we choose to believe in Jesus. This is also faith. We should
put our whole faith and trust in Jesus, because the Bible says that
this is the only way we can be saved.

REFLECT

Write down three reasons you know Jesus is real in your life.

_____

_____

_____

WHAT IT MEANS
TO BELIEVE IN GOD, FOR REAL

[GOD:] "But my righteous one will live by faith.
And I take no pleasure in the one who shrinks back."

[US:] But we do not belong to those who shrink back and
are destroyed, but to those who have faith and are saved.

HEBREWS 10:38–39

Believing in God is a decision that means no matter what we hear, read, or see—and no matter what others may say to us to try and change our beliefs—we choose to believe in God/Jesus. We choose to live our lives by faith. Living by faith means that every day, our decisions, actions, and thoughts come from a place of knowing that God and His Word, the Bible, are real.

You may have friends or teachers who believe in entirely different gods, or that there is no God at all. Some may try to persuade you to believe like them one day. But when you believe in God, for real, it means you've resolved in your heart that NOTHING can convince you otherwise. When you get information that seems contrary to God and Jesus, question that information, not your God. Then you'll know that your faith is strong, and you will never shrink back.

REFLECT

Write down something that might make someone doubt that God is real—it could be something you've heard from other kids, at school, or online, or you could just use your imagination. Then take it to a pastor or church leader and ask them about it. See what you can come up with together to show how that thing shouldn't come against someone's faith in God.

_____

_____

_____

KNOWING GOD

All Scripture is God-breathed and is useful for teaching,
rebuking, correcting and training in righteousness,
so that the servant of God may be thoroughly
equipped for every good work.

2 TIMOTHY 3:16–17

The Bible is a really big book! It can be intimidating to read it if
you don't know where to begin. Before reading the Bible, it's really
important to know its purpose. This will help you understand
it better.

Have you ever heard that B.I.B.L.E. is an acronym for "Basic
Instructions Before Leaving Earth"? Although the Bible really does
provide us with instructions, direction, and guidance and helps us
know what God wants for our lives, this is actually not its *main* purpose. The Bible's main purpose is to help us know and understand
God better.

If you read the Bible regularly, it's easier to look at any situation
in your life and know what God's heart and thoughts about it might
be. This is so important, because God created you (and everything
in the universe) and knows the absolute best things for your life!
Wouldn't you want to know what your Creator thinks?

REFLECT

Want to read the Bible but don't know where to start? Read Luke and Acts
(the story of Jesus and His disciples), Ephesians (a letter the Apostle Paul
wrote to a church), and James, 1 John, and 1 Timothy. James, 1 John, and
1 Timothy are all great books to help strengthen young people like you.

Write the first two books you'd like to read below and why you picked each
of them.

GOD'S LOVE IS GUARANTEED

For I am convinced that neither death nor life, neither
angels nor demons, neither the present nor the future,
nor any powers, neither height nor depth, nor anything
else in all creation, will be able to separate us from
the love of God that is in Christ Jesus our Lord.

ROMANS 8:38–39

Have you ever done something wrong and worried that God, or
maybe even your parents, didn't love you as much in that moment?
You might have thought, *How could they love me? I've disappointed them so badly.* Well, you don't have to worry about that.
The verses above show that there is literally nothing in the whole
universe, natural or spiritual, that can stop God from loving us.

Much like the love of our parents and guardians, God's love is
unconditional. That means God loves you no matter what happens.
There is nothing you can do that will stop God from loving you!
His love is "guaranteed." Isn't that great to know? Just like a good
parent, God simply asks us to repent when we've done wrong. You
can ask God to forgive you and help you do the right thing from
now on. If this all seems a bit overwhelming, you can ask a parent
to help you with this.

REFLECT

What are some ways you can remind yourself of God's unconditional love?
Try to brainstorm three ideas. For example, you could write a note to yourself like "God loves you no matter what!" and stick it on your mirror, keep
it on your dresser, or even make a screen saver out of it. It will be a great
reminder when you're feeling low!

_____

_____

_____

LOVING OTHERS

A new command I give you: Love one another.
As I have loved you, so you must love one another.

JOHN 13:34

Most of us have wondered what it really means to "love one another." It can be especially hard when the people around us, like siblings or other family members, aren't being very lovable. If you're confused about love, you can look to Jesus, who was an amazing example of love. He loved by making the greatest sacrifice—not only did Jesus live for us, but He also died on the cross for us. By doing so, He forgave you and me. He even forgave the people who were crucifying Him, because He knew God created them and loved them, too. He made the greatest sacrifice anyone could make for another, and He instructs us to love others the *same* way He loved us.

Now, is Jesus asking us to die for others? Not necessarily. But He is instructing us to see others the way He sees them, and to recognize that God made all of us and loves everyone the same. He wants us to love one another with the love of God. This means being willing to get uncomfortable in order to treat others in the loving and merciful way Jesus has treated us. This can be difficult sometimes. But the next time you start getting upset with someone, think of what the love of Jesus would look like in that situation. Then try and let that thought guide your actions.

REFLECT

Write down a few ways you can sacrifice to love the people around you. How would Jesus want you to love them?

_____

_____

_____

YOUR PARENTS ARE ON YOUR SIDE

Listen, my son, to your father's instruction and do not
forsake your mother's teaching. They are a garland to
grace your head and a chain to adorn your neck.

PROVERBS 1:8–9

Does it ever feel like your parents or guardians ask you to behave in
ways that just don't make sense to you? Maybe they tell you to do
things you really wish you didn't have to do, or forbid you to do stuff
you want to do. In the Bible, God instructs His followers to listen to
and obey their authority figures. It's one way He shows love to them,
by protecting them.

Even when it seems like your parents or guardians aren't on your
side, remember that they love you and want what's right for you. If
you're finding that tough to understand, think about a time when
you were corrected or disciplined for something you didn't think
was wrong but later found out was dangerous or bad for you, like
playing in an area where you could have fallen or been injured.

Your parents and guardians will always be there, no matter how
badly you behave. They'll be there to love you, discipline you, and
get you on the right track. The Bible also has a bonus promise:
When you obey your parents, you will have a long life full of good
things (Ephesians 6:1–3)!

REFLECT

Has your parent or guardian been on you lately about doing something that
you really don't like to do? Write about the reasons they may have for asking
you to do it. Then try doing that thing this week without being asked, and
see how much easier that part of your life gets.

_____

_____

_____

YOU DON'T HAVE TO FEEL ANXIOUS

Do not be anxious about anything, but in every situation, by prayer and petition, with thanksgiving, present your requests to God. And the peace of God, which transcends all understanding, will guard your hearts and your minds in Christ Jesus.

PHILIPPIANS 4:6–7

We all would love to live a life where we are always happy and peaceful. But life doesn't always feel that way. Sometimes, we have moments of worry that make us feel anxious. This feeling of anxiety comes from the thought that bad things could happen and there's nothing you can do to stop them. But you don't have to fear, because God is with you.

You might be feeling anxious about a big test, an upcoming sports event, or even a difficult talk you have to have with parents or friends. But God tells us in His Word not to worry or be anxious. You don't need to be scared, because God is always watching over you and taking care of you.

When you are anxious, you can get peace by doing three things:

1. Remember what God has promised to you in His Word.
2. Pray and ask for God's help.
3. Thank God for His goodness and remember how good He has already been.

REFLECT

Think about a recent time when you were worried about what might happen. How could you have used these three steps to calm your fears?

IF YOU WANT FRUIT, PLANT SEEDS

But the fruit of the Spirit is love, joy, peace, forbearance,
kindness, goodness, faithfulness, gentleness and self-control.
Against such things there is no law.

GALATIANS 5:22–23

In order to grow the fruit that we eat, we must plant seeds. To get
an apple tree, we plant apple seeds, right? It's the same for the fruit
of the Spirit. In order to get "Spirit fruit," we must plant "Spirit seeds."
The Spirit here is referring to the Holy Spirit (God's Spirit). You can
plant Spirit seeds simply by spending time with God: reading the
Bible and other Christian books (like this one!), worshiping, watching Christian shows, going to church and learning about God, and
even having godly conversations with friends and family members.

It's so easy to plant these seeds if you just take the time. Sometimes, that means stepping away from friends, video games, TV,
and other screens. Just like you have to spend time with a friend to
get to know them better, if you want to get closer to God, you must
give Him your time. If you make time for God, before you know
it, you will have all kinds of Spirit fruit: love, joy, peace, kindness,
self-control, and more!

REFLECT

Can you think of any other ways to plant seeds of the Spirit? Jot them down
here and try some out this week. See what kind of fruit you can grow!

_____

_____

_____

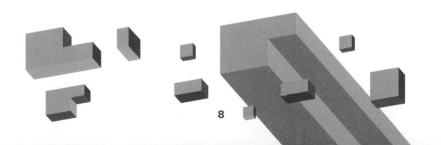

PRAYING GOD'S WILL

This is the confidence we have in approaching God: that if
we ask anything according to his will, he hears us.
And if we know that he hears us—whatever
we ask—we know that we have what we asked of him.

1 JOHN 5:14–15

Sometimes when we pray, we may wonder whether God hears us. But we don't have to wonder. The Bible tells us that if we ask anything that is according to God's will, He hears us and answers our prayers. Notice, however, that the requirement is that we pray His will. How do we know whether it's God's will? If what we are asking in prayer lines up with what we see from God's Word and His character, then that's usually God's will. That's why it's so important to continue to learn more and more about God and His Word.

Sometimes, we want to pray for the newest gaming console or to be invited to someone's birthday party. But what if that's not God's will for your life? Do you still want it? We need to desire what God wants for our lives. If you do, you will have the best life and be able to live according to God's purpose for you. Once you pray, remember to be patient. God will answer your prayers in His best timing.

REFLECT

If you're currently praying for something to happen in your life (or another person's), ask yourself, "Is this according to God's will?" Write your answer below. If you're not sure, write your prayer down, then ask someone who really knows the Bible (like a parent or church leader/teacher) about it. See whether you can find something about your prayer in God's Word. Write the scripture along with your prayer, and start praying according to God's Word and will. Then be patient, knowing that God hears you and is answering your prayers.

BEING A GOOD INFLUENCE

Don't let anyone look down on you because you are
young, but set an example for the believers in speech,
in conduct, in love, in faith and in purity.

1 TIMOTHY 4:12

When you hear the term "role model," you might think of a great
athlete or your favorite movie star. But did you know that we are all
role models? It's true! We are all role models, because we all have
influence. Influence is basically the way you affect someone else,
through your words and actions. And you have a lot of influence,
even if you don't know it—you can even influence someone without saying anything, just through the things that you do. When you
think of influence, you might think about adults like parents, teachers, celebrities, and coaches. But we all have the power to influence
others, regardless of our age.

The Bible tells us that we should use our influence to help others
learn to do the right thing. This means you can influence your
friends, classmates, and siblings by setting a good example. When
you are kind to others at school, respectful to teachers, and careful
with your words, you are using your power of influence for good.

Ask God to help you set a good example for others today, in all
that you say and do. When you do this, God will be pleased, and
you will make the world better, one person at a time.

REFLECT

In what way can you set a good example for your siblings? Your friends?
Your peers? People whom you don't know? Jot some ideas down and try to
put them into action this week.

_____

_____

_____

LIVING IN GENEROSITY

For God so loved the world that he gave his one
and only Son, that whoever believes in him shall
not perish but have eternal life.

JOHN 3:16

When you hear about giving, you might think about the way your
family gives at church. But did you know that generosity is not just
about money? You can be generous with your time, your talents,
your effort, your belongings, and even yourself. We see in the Bible
verse above that God was generous with His most prized possession:
His only son. Imagine how much He must love us all to give us the
most important thing He had! God wants us to be generous, like Him.
He wants us to love others enough to give them our absolute best.

Being generous just means that you are willing to sacrifice
whatever you *do* have in order to give. Being generous is a lifestyle:
something you do all the time.

PRAYER

*Lord, I want to be generous like You. Please help me be willing to
make sacrifices for others, and help me see when others have
a need that I can fill. Thank You for making me more and more
like You each day. I love You. In Jesus's name, amen.*

REFLECT

Take a moment to imagine giving your most prized possession away to
someone else. Does it make you feel a little sad or uneasy to lose it? Maybe
you feel happy to share something so awesome. This is only a small taste
of how God felt when He gave Jesus. Write down some of the feelings you
felt when you imagined this, as well as a few things you can do for others or
give to others this week.

GOD'S STRENGTH HELPS
US GET THROUGH ANYTHING

I can do all this through him who gives me strength.

PHILIPPIANS 4:13

When something gets hard, it's normal to feel like you just can't do it. Sometimes, you might not be able to see how you'll ever make it through a difficult situation. When the Apostle Paul wrote the book of Philippians, he was going through some really tough times. But he let people know that because he had the help of God (through Jesus Christ), he absolutely knew he could do *anything* God wanted him to.

God wants you to get through the difficult times, and He's always there to help you. Just trust in Him and ask Him for help, and He will walk you through it.

God is always on your side, rooting for you and strengthening you in the process. Remember this: No matter how hard life gets, you can always call on the Lord, Jesus, and He will be by your side, just like He was with Paul.

PRAYER

*Father God, I need strength right now. Please help me know that
I can get through this and that I can get through anything.
Thank You for Your help, Your guidance, and Your strength.
In Jesus's name, amen.*

REFLECT

Is there something you're going through right now that seems like it's a little too tough for you to deal with on your own? Write it here and ask a family member or church leader to pray about it with you. Then agree to talk regularly to see how it's going.

_____

_____

_____

EXPECT GOOD THINGS

"For I know the plans I have for you," declares the LORD,
"plans to prosper you and not to harm you, plans to
give you hope and a future."

JEREMIAH 29:11

Have you ever watched a movie where things looked so hopeless
for the main character, you thought there was no possible way they
were going to make it? It seemed like all hope was lost, until, mirac-
ulously, things turned around. It can be hard to have hope when
things around you seem hopeless. But with God on your side, you
never have to feel hopeless or helpless. He always has a great plan
for your turnaround. How do you get to this great plan? Expect
good things—in other words, put your hope in God.

Hope is simply a confident expectation. It's knowing that something good is going to happen, because God is with you. This is
what the Lord instructed Jeremiah to write to His people, who
were being oppressed. Things weren't looking good for them, and
they were losing hope. But He knew they had to keep their hope in
God, because without it, things would fall apart. Hope in God leads
to faith in God. And faith in God allows God to do great things in
our lives.

Even if school isn't going well, or you're not getting along with
your friends, God still has a great plan for you. Just trust Him. You
can show your trust in God by expecting good things.

REFLECT

Is there an area in your life where you need to put your hope in God again?
Write that area down below. Then tell God that you expect good things to
happen in this area, and prepare to see them happen.

_____

_____

_____

BEING CONFIDENT

The fruit of that righteousness will be peace;
its effect will be quietness and confidence forever.

ISAIAH 32:17

One of the greatest strengths you can have in life is confidence. Confident people are bold about who they are and what they stand for. Sometimes, people with confidence seem like they know something that the rest of us don't.

The great thing about knowing God is that He gives us access to confidence through Jesus. Because we are right with God, we can have confidence in whatever we face. The key to true confidence is knowing that you are special to God! When you know that you are special, you also know that you have something great to offer others.

Only you can decide whether you are going to have confidence. Many times, doubt will try to come into your mind and make you second-guess yourself. That's exactly what the devil wants you to do—doubt yourself. So remember that you are amazing, and God made you that way. Don't doubt yourself. When you're around a group of kids whom you don't know, speak with confidence. When you're not sure whether you have the right answer in class, raise your hand and answer the question with boldness. So what if you're wrong? With God on your side, you will be able to stand up to anything that life has to offer.

REFLECT

Think of someone you admire who is confident. What do they do that shows you they have confidence? What can you do to display more confidence?

_____

_____

_____

WHEN SOMEONE HAS WRONGED YOU

Be kind and compassionate to one another, forgiving
each other, just as in Christ God forgave you.

EPHESIANS 4:32

When someone hurts you or does something mean to you, it can be really difficult to even think about forgiving them. Sometimes, you might feel like you want to hurt them back. But God's Word tells us that we must forgive. Did you know forgiveness is an act of love? And love is the most powerful thing in the universe. As a matter of fact, the Bible also says that God is love. When we forgive others, we are putting God right in the middle of our situation.

God doesn't want you to get revenge. God can heal your pain and frustration, if you let Him. That's why when you forgive someone who hurts you, it makes *you* feel better. After you forgive the other person, pray for them so God can do a work in them, too.

Note: If someone is hurting you regularly, be sure to talk to a trusted adult about it. Although forgiveness is important, your safety is important, too, and the people who care about you want to keep you safe from harm.

PRAYER

Lord, I want to forgive _____. Please help me forgive them, even though they _____. Thank You that I have forgiven them and that You are healing my heart. In Jesus's name, amen.

REFLECT

Write down the names of the people you need to forgive and then pray the prayer above for each one. Share how this made you feel with someone you trust, so they can help you through this process.

_____

_____

_____

THE MOST VALUABLE THING

How much better to get wisdom than gold,
to get insight rather than silver!

PROVERBS 16:16

In difficult situations, the first thing that you should do is get wisdom. We get wisdom by asking God for it. God says that wisdom is one of the most valuable things you could ever get or ask for from Him. That's because when you don't know what to do, God does. When we ask for the wisdom of God, He is able to provide us with answers we could never have figured out on our own. The wisdom that God gives us leads to peace and many other good things.

The Scripture reminds us that wisdom was with God when He created the earth, helping Him do it in the best way possible. Wisdom can help you find solutions to complicated problems, work through a disagreement with a friend, or even be creative in your school projects.

The great thing about wisdom is that God says He will give it to us freely whenever we need it. All you have to do is ask!

PRAYER

*Father, give me Your wisdom today so I can know exactly
what to think, what to do, and how to do it. In Jesus's name, amen.*

REFLECT

Write down a few situations in your life in which wisdom could benefit you.

_____

_____

_____

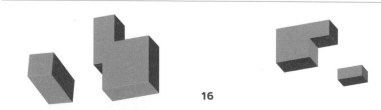

HAVE COURAGE

Have I not commanded you? Be strong and courageous.
Do not be afraid; do not be discouraged, for the LORD
your God will be with you wherever you go.

JOSHUA 1:9

The first year of high school, I moved to a new town with my family. I was nervous about starting school, because all the other students had been together in elementary and middle school, while I was the new kid. I tried my best to fit in.

Later that fall, they announced basketball tryouts. I really loved playing basketball, but I had never been on a school team, and I didn't think I would make it if I tried out. I was afraid to play in front of so many people I didn't know. But a small voice inside said, "Go for it, David." I asked God to give me courage, and He did. I went to the tryouts the following week and discovered I had made the team!

When God told Joshua that it was time to go into the Promised Land, Joshua was scared, too. He knew that there were giants in that land. But God reminded him just like He reminds us: "I am always with you." And Joshua was able to lead his people into the Promised Land and defeat the other armies.

As you grow into manhood, you will face a lot of challenges. It will take courage to face your fears. The secret to finding courage is remembering that God is with you wherever you go. And when God is with you, you can face anything.

REFLECT

Write down three things that you can do or say to remind yourself that God is always with you.

_____

_____

_____

GRACE AND JESUS'S SACRIFICE

For it is by grace you have been saved, through faith—and
this is not from yourselves, it is the gift of God—not by
works, so that no one can boast.

EPHESIANS 2:8-9

Grace is God's goodness that gives us access to things that we don't deserve. Receiving the grace of God is not about how good our behavior is; it's a free gift from God that we can only get by faith. Even on our best day, we could never *earn* healing, blessings, prosperity, favor, salvation, and God's love. Because of Jesus's sacrifice, we were rescued from pain, sin, and bondage. That's why no one can claim that their moral actions saved them. None of us deserved this grace, yet all of us can have it. All we have to do is believe in Jesus.

When the Apostle Paul wrote the passage above, he saw that young Christians were trying to earn God's salvation by doing good deeds. But salvation can't be earned, because it has nothing to do with what you have done. For example, when someone gives you a gift, they don't make you earn that gift before giving it to you. They bought it with you in mind, and they want you to have it, no matter what you've done. The grace of God works the same way. Salvation is something special that God purchased for us, through the sacrifice of Jesus on the cross. To receive it, all we have to do is believe in Jesus.

Why does God do all of this? It's because of His amazing love for us and His kindness that we can experience this grace.

REFLECT

What's the best thing about God? Does He make you earn that? Or does He give it freely, regardless of how you act?

BUT EVERYBODY'S DOING IT

My son, if sinful men entice you, do not give in
to them . . . do not go along with them, do not set foot
on their paths; for their feet rush into evil . . .

PROVERBS 1:10, 15–16A

It can feel very hard when you're the only one doing the right thing. But it's especially hard when the people who are misbehaving are your friends—and when they're asking you to join them in their bad behavior. Pressure from your peers, including friends, classmates, and other people your age, can be very powerful and tough to resist. They may encourage you to do things that your parents have told you not to do, that the Word of God specifically says are wrong, or that your conscience or the Holy Spirit tells you are what you shouldn't be doing. Times like these are when you must resist peer pressure.

When we choose friends, we are basically saying, "These are the people I want to have influence in my life." But what if you're choosing the wrong friends? In 1 Corinthians 15:33 (NKJV), the Bible says, "Do not be deceived: 'Evil company corrupts good habits.'" When you have the wrong people around you, they can affect your behavior. Pay close attention to whom you are allowing into your life. Don't "walk" with people who have a reputation for running toward evil. Instead, be the person "pressuring" others to do good.

REFLECT

On the lines below, write one list of the friends who influence you to do good things and another of the friends who pressure you to do things you know are wrong. Then show this list to an adult you trust and discuss ways you can resist peer pressure to do wrong things.

LIVING LIKE JESUS

Greater love has no one than this:
to lay down one's life for one's friends.

JOHN 15:13

Jesus literally laid down His life for His friends—friends like you
and me. It's what He came to do: to sacrifice His life, so that we
might have life and live it to the fullest. Numerous times in the
Bible, Jesus asks us to live like Him, love like Him, serve like
Him, and sacrifice like Him. He's our example of what it means
to sacrifice.

But Jesus isn't asking us to die on a cross—that's not the only
sacrifice Jesus made. Jesus always put others first. He served and
cared for people when He was tired, hungry, and sad. Even when
He barely had anything left, He gave what He had to others. He was
always giving, helping, and teaching. His life was lived for other
people. And sometimes, that made Him very unpopular. That's
what it means to sacrifice: living to benefit others, even when
it's difficult.

We can copy the ways Jesus sacrificed in His daily life. For you,
this may mean helping a family member with chores without being
asked, instead of playing a game or chatting with your friends. It
could also mean sticking up for someone whom your friends aren't
being very nice to. It could be anything that doesn't necessarily
sound fun but that you know would help others.

REFLECT

What is the most difficult thing you ever decided to do for someone? Was it
a service? Giving something away? Not taking something so someone else
could have it? Write down what you did and how you felt after you did it.

DOING YOUR BEST

Serve wholeheartedly, as if you were serving the Lord,
not people, because you know that the Lord will reward
each one for whatever good they do . . .

EPHESIANS 6:7–8

Sometimes, you have to do things that you don't feel like doing—things like chores, homework, or practicing an instrument. And it's okay that you don't feel like doing them. But in His Word, God commands us to do our work with all our heart.

What if God Himself came to you and asked you to do the task you don't feel like doing? You would do your absolute best, right? Well, that's how God asks you to look at it—as if you were doing the work not just for the person who asked you to do it, but for Him. He says that He will reward you for a job well done. In everything you do, God asks you to do your best, because in the end, it's Him you are serving, and your work reflects God's goodness.

REFLECT

Are there any areas of your life where you could try harder? School, chores, or getting along with your siblings? Write it down below. And the next time you have to do something in that area, decide to do your absolute best! Jot down how you felt afterward as well.

_____

_____

_____

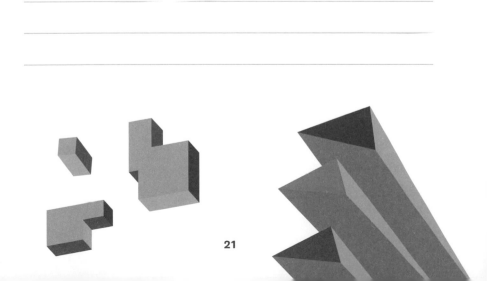

WHY WE GO TO CHURCH

And let us consider how we may spur one another on toward love and good deeds, not giving up meeting together, as some are in the habit of doing, but encouraging one another . . .

HEBREWS 10:24–25A

Church is a really important part of Christian life. At church, you gather with your brothers and sisters in Christ—your other family. With this family, you learn how to love and serve one another, as well as other people outside the church. You also encourage one another. You are taught the Word of God so that you grow in Christ. And you get to show the Lord some love by praising Him and talking about Him with other Christians.

In His Word, God asks us to not let anything stop us from meeting up with one another. So even when you want to sleep in on Sundays or go play with friends, remember that the best way we can honor this request is by going to church.

REFLECT

What does church mean for your faith and for your life? Write down some of the reasons why going to church is so important for you.

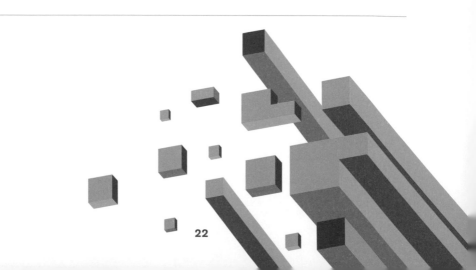

BECOMING THE FRIEND
YOU WISH YOU HAD

Do to others as you would have them do to you.

LUKE 6:31

If you closed your eyes and pictured the perfect friend, what would they be like? They'd be supportive, caring, fun, and smart, right? They would stick with you through anything. When something goes wrong, they don't leave—they want to work it out. Maybe they aren't actually even perfect, but they treat you like *you* are.

You probably spend a lot of time thinking about what kind of friends you want to have. But it's also really important to think about the kind of friend you want to be. Jesus tells us to treat other people the way we want to be treated. You should always be growing and developing into the best version of yourself, and that includes becoming a better friend. Be the kind of friend that you would want to have.

REFLECT

Take a moment and write down all the qualities you would want in a friend. Now look at each one and ask yourself, "Does this describe me?" Think of one quality you'd like to become better at—say, listening to people's problems—and think of one way you could work to get better at it.

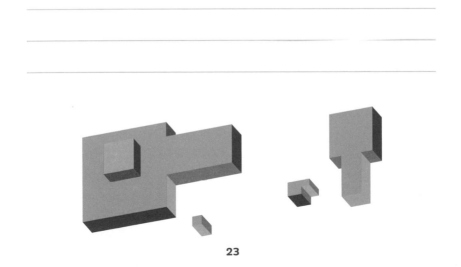

SECURITY IN CHRIST

*You, dear children, are from God and have
overcome them, because the one who is in you is
greater than the one who is in the world.*

1 JOHN 4:4

When you walk through an automatic door, it doesn't matter how
tall you are, how smart you are, what grades you get, or how well
you play basketball. As long as you stand in the right position, the
door will open and let you in. It's the same with God: It doesn't
matter who you are, what you've done, or what you look like. You
have no reason to feel insecure. There is no fear of judgment. You
are secure in God's sacrifice and love. And because of that, you can
go through life with confidence, becoming more secure because
you know who Jesus is and who He is inside of you.

Since you have this security with God, you don't have to be
insecure about who you are or what you stand for. You don't need
anyone or anything to make you feel significant. You are important because you are in Christ, a part of the family of God, the most
royal family in the universe. When you are secure and confident
in who you are, you can face everything with confidence—school,
friendships, sports, you name it. So go through the day
with confidence!

REFLECT

What are three areas where God can help you grow in confidence? Write
them below. Some ideas: speaking up at school, playing sports, working
hard at a school subject you struggle with, meeting new friends, and being
bold about being a Christian.

_____

_____

_____

FORGIVENESS OVER JUDGMENT

Do not judge, and you will not be judged. Do not condemn, and you will not be condemned. Forgive, and you will be forgiven.

LUKE 6:37

Have you ever had someone who you thought was a friend do something really mean? You may have felt so hurt that you decided that you were just finished being friends with them. But that's not God's way. Instead of giving people what they deserved for their wrongdoings, God sent Jesus to forgive everyone. That's what He wants from us, too. God doesn't want you to judge others. He wants you to forgive them.

Judging others is when you decide to have a bad opinion about someone, even when you don't know much about their situation. You might see someone who doesn't look very clean and assume they are scary or a bad person. But you may see that same person the next day all cleaned up and realize that they were just doing some yard work. Or remember that friend who was mean? What if you found out they were going through a really hard time at home and took it out on you without thinking? Instead of being quick to judge, maybe you should have tried to learn more, then understand and forgive them.

When we judge others, we are often incorrect about them and don't see the full picture. Sometimes, we forget that God made each of us in His image, He loves us all equally, and we are all important *to Him*. That's why God doesn't want us to judge. He wants us to see one another as He sees us.

REFLECT

Are there some people you should focus on forgiving instead of judging? Write their names below and see whether you can spend some time this week trying to understand them better.

_____

_____

_____

WHY GOD MADE YOU

Each of you should use whatever gift you have received
to serve others, as faithful stewards of God's grace in its
various forms. If anyone speaks, they should do so as
one who speaks the very words of God. If anyone serves,
they should do so with the strength God provides, so
that in all things God may be praised through Jesus Christ.
To him be the glory and the power for ever and ever. Amen.

1 PETER 4:10–11

God gave each and every one of us a gift. He gave us special talents that we can use to serve others and glorify Him. You may ask
yourself, "What is my gift? I'm not musical, artistic, or particularly
athletic." But that doesn't mean that you don't have a gift. Some
of our gifts are not as visible as others, and that's okay. Are you
good at taking care of your siblings? Maybe you have a knack for
understanding others really well, or perhaps you're great with tech-
nology. Whatever you do, you should do it for God, knowing that
He gave you the power to do it and to benefit other people. Why?
The Bible says it's so God can get the glory through Jesus Christ.

Because you're a Christian, when you use your gifts to help other
people, you spread His name and His Word. You're helping Jesus
with His command for us to "make disciples." It is exciting to know
that you are made for God's purpose and that you can help Him
with His plan, no matter how young you are. What a gift it is to be
able to serve God!

REFLECT

What makes you special? Write some things you're good at, and think about
ways you can glorify God with your unique gifts.

_____

_____

_____

GRATITUDE MAKES YOU HAPPY

I know what it is to be in need, and I know what it is to
have plenty. I have learned the secret of being content
in any and every situation, whether well fed or hungry,
whether living in plenty or in want. I can do all this
through him who gives me strength.

PHILIPPIANS 4:12–13

It can be hard to have a good attitude when you're not getting what
you want. The Apostle Paul certainly understood that. But he also
knew how to always be content, whether or not he had everything
he needed or wanted. He learned to be grateful for what God did in
his life, and that gratitude provided him with strength and happiness in times of want.

When we are grateful—and especially when we're grateful for
what God has done for us—it's so much easier to be happy. It's easy
to adjust your attitude; it just takes your participation. This means
that, like Paul, you must *decide* that you will be content in any and
every situation.

REFLECT

Think of five things you are grateful for. Write them down below. And the
next time you feel a bad attitude coming on, go back to this list and thank
God for everything on it.

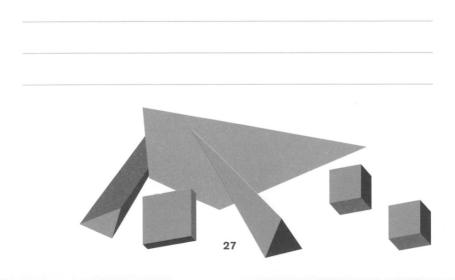

27

THE BEST THING YOU CAN DO

Now that I, your Lord and Teacher, have washed your feet,
you also should wash one another's feet. I have set you
an example that you should do as I have done for you.

JOHN 13:14–15

Have you ever had someone help you out when you didn't expect it? It was probably a nice surprise that put a smile on your face. Whether it is helping a classmate with an assignment or volunteering at church, giving a helping hand makes life better.

When Jesus was preparing to go to the cross, He decided to have one last meal with His closest friends, the disciples. During that meal, He shared many things from His heart. But there was one message that He wanted them to really remember: the message of serving others. He wanted them to remember it so much that He washed their feet, so they would see an example. Jesus didn't *have* to wash the disciples' feet, which were probably dirty and stinky. But that was just the point—Jesus wanted to do something that they did not expect and could not repay Him for. Jesus wanted us to remember not to be so focused on ourselves that we forget to give others a helping hand. This is God's will for us, too.

REFLECT

What are some nice things that you can do for others at home? At school? What about something nice that you can do for a teacher or coach? List a few ideas below.

_____

_____

_____

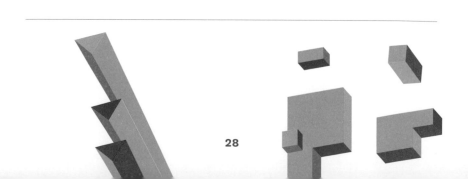

IT'S NOT JUST ABOUT THE GRADES

Whatever you do, work at it with all your heart, as working
for the Lord, not for human masters, since you know that
you will receive an inheritance from the Lord as a reward.
It is the Lord Christ you are serving.

COLOSSIANS 3:23–24

Whether you are a good student who always gets good grades
or someone who is having a hard time in school right now, God
requires the same thing from all of us: our best effort. It's not just
about getting a good grade. It's also about pleasing the Lord with
the effort that you give when working toward that good grade.

Whenever we give our best effort, God says that we will receive
a reward. Every time you work hard, God is pleased. Being a good
student is not just about the grade you get, it's about what the
grades get out of you—your best effort.

So don't give up. Even if you are having trouble with a certain
subject, keep trying to understand. Your hard work will pay off.
And even if you don't get the A grade that you were hoping for,
don't feel bad—God is still pleased with your effort. Working with
"all of your heart" is what God is looking for. When you give your
best effort, you make your teachers, your parents, and, most of all,
God proud.

REFLECT

Think about the effort that you put in at school and on your assignments. On
a scale of 1 to 10, with 1 being poor and 10 being amazing, how would you
grade your effort? What are some ways that you can increase your effort?

CHOOSING YOUR FRIENDS CAREFULLY

As iron sharpens iron, so one person sharpens another.

PROVERBS 27:17

Choosing the right friends can make your life so much better. Spending time with friends who are smart, loving, wise, and good-hearted will cause you to become smarter, wiser, more loving, and more good-hearted. It goes the other way, too—the Bible says that negative friendships will corrupt you. One verse tells us not to make friends with an angry man, because you'll get caught up in his ways and get in trouble, too.

Sometimes, friendships end, and we may or may not know why they ended. But don't be discouraged. Perhaps that friendship was not sharpening you. God has a plan, and a new friend is around the corner. Instead of feeling upset, be on the lookout for the new friends whom God has put in front of you.

When it comes to friends, you have choices. And God shows us in His Word how important it is that you choose wisely. You don't have to be close friends with just any person who comes along. Instead, be careful and conscious about it. Become closely connected to the people you know God has put in your life to make it better—and to make *you* better.

REFLECT

Think about your good friends, and write down some of their godly characteristics. Can you think of any other people who share some of those qualities and might be good, godly friends for you? If you can, try to get their contact information and maybe even reach out to one of them. If you can't, brainstorm some activities you could join to meet more people with those qualities.

_____

_____

_____

SERVING OTHERS

When he had finished washing their feet, he . . . returned
to his place. "Do you understand what I have done for you?"
he asked them . . . "Now that I, your Lord and Teacher, have
washed your feet, you also should wash one another's feet."

JOHN 13:12, 14

Jesus commands us to love and serve others. Does He want you
to wash people's feet? Not necessarily. What He was trying to help
us understand is that sometimes, really serving others may involve
doing things that you don't feel like doing, or that may seem
"beneath" you. When serving others, Jesus humbled Himself and
did some of the lowest things people could do for one another at
that time. He even died on the cross to serve humanity.

Jesus gave people what they needed, and He wants you to serve
others like He did. When you serve others, the question to ask
yourself and God is "What do they need?" God will help you understand what people need, and He will help you have the strength to
fill their need. Serving like Jesus means looking out for the needs of
others, even when it's a sacrifice. This might include doing things
like helping a friend with homework, doing a family member's
least-favorite chore, volunteering to do yard work for an elderly
neighbor, or taking on a responsibility that is not yours at church
or at sports practice. All of this helps us get closer to God.

REFLECT

Over the next few days, ask all the members of your family, "How can I serve
you better?" Jot down their answers below and try to fulfill some of their
requests this week.

_____

_____

_____

REAL LEADERS HELP OTHERS LEAD

After this the Lord appointed seventy-two others and
sent them two by two ahead of him to every town
and place where he was about to go.

LUKE 10:1

Have you ever been part of a team where the leader did everything themselves and wouldn't let you do anything at all? It probably felt frustrating, because you just wanted to help. Good leaders don't do everything themselves. Instead, they let others help out and show them how to lead.

Even when Jesus walked this earth, He didn't do everything by himself; He had to depend on the help of His disciples. When He sent them ahead to the next town to prepare people for His coming, the disciples had to trust that Jesus knew what He was doing when He sent them on, and Jesus had to be confident that He had prepared the disciples for any difficulties that they would face along the way. Jesus performed many miracles, but the work of the disciples made His impact even greater. Jesus's leadership prepared the disciples to lead.

As disciples of Christ, our mission is like the mission of Jesus. We are here to do God's will, but we are also here to show others how to lead. We are all important to God's plan. He doesn't want anyone left out. Just as Jesus told us to go and make disciples, I say to you, "Go and make leaders."

REFLECT

Think about the best team that you have been a part of. Who was the leader of that team? What did they do well that made the team so good?

DON'T YOU DARE COMPARE

We do not dare to classify or compare ourselves
with some who commend themselves. When they
measure themselves by themselves and compare
themselves with themselves, they are not wise.

2 CORINTHIANS 10:12

In school, you probably sometimes get assignments that ask you to compare two different things—two sentences, two math equations, two pictures. Many times, the goal is to find which one is correct or *better*. This means the other option is *wrong*. Sometimes, we can be tempted to look at ourselves the same way, comparing ourselves with friends or other peers. You may be tempted to think that they are better than you, which makes you feel bad about yourself. Or you might do the opposite and think that you are better than them.

God does not want us to think that way. We are His creation, made special and unique, just the way He wanted us. In the Bible, God warns us about the temptation to compare ourselves with others. He knows that it is not wise, because it can make us feel sad and frustrated, or even make us think we are better than others. As we are all one in Christ's body, God made us to fit together perfectly, like puzzle pieces coming together. No two pieces are the same, but each one is needed to complete the puzzle.

You are just as valuable as your friend, peer, or favorite YouTuber. Yes, you are different, but that's what makes you awesome. Be proud that you are different. You are the best one at being you!

REFLECT

What are the things that make you unique or special? Think about how those things benefit the people around you.

_____

_____

_____

HAVE YOU EVER FELT ANGRY?

Refrain from anger and turn from wrath;
do not fret—it leads only to evil.

PSALM 37:8

Can you remember a time when you felt angry because things didn't go your way? Maybe you got in trouble for something that was not your fault. Or maybe someone took something of yours and wouldn't give it back. Don't worry, it's normal to feel angry sometimes. But anger can come with a negative feeling of frustration inside that can be hard to control. Did you know that feelings travel 80,000 times faster than thoughts? Because feelings travel so much faster, it's easy to let them take control, instead of thinking coolly about the next best step.

In the Bible, David writes about anger and how to handle it. A man named King Saul was trying to hurt him, and David didn't even know why. But he knew that it was important to control his emotions. If he gave in to his feelings of anger, he would not be able to control himself. He might even want to hurt King Saul. He knew that acting on anger could lead to something bad.

The next time you feel angry, stop and take five deep breaths. Ask yourself, "What can I control?" You may not be able to control what others are saying or doing, but you can always control how you react. When you focus on positive things, it will help you change your feelings in the moment.

REFLECT

Write down two things that make you angry. Then write down some positive things that you can focus on the next time you get angry.

_____

_____

_____

LOVING YOUR BULLIES

But I tell you, love your enemies
and pray for those who persecute you.

MATTHEW 5:44

Have you ever been mistreated not because of anything you did, but because of who you are, how you look, or where you are from? Did you know that Jesus himself experienced bullying? Some people celebrated him, but many others made fun of him. They said that nothing good could come from Nazareth, the place Jesus called home.

Normally, when we are bullied, we become afraid, sad, and angry. Not Jesus, though. Instead of reacting in fear and anger, Jesus chose to respond to his bullies with love and prayer. You might be wondering, "How did that help Him?" The Bible says that God is love, and when we choose to walk in love toward others, we allow God to get involved in our situation. And when God and His love are involved, we don't have to be afraid, angry, or sad.

When you love and pray for your bullies, you can stand up for yourself, because you are no longer afraid. Instead of hiding, you can take the information to parents, teachers, or other leaders. Invite God in through prayer, and feel the love and courage He provides. Know that you are not alone.

PRAYER

Lord, I pray for those who are mistreating me. Help me find courage and comfort in Your love for me, and help me show them the same love that You have shown me. Bless them and help them. In Jesus's name, amen.

REFLECT

Jot down some ways you can show love to a bully who is bothering you. You could give them a cool pencil, a compliment, or even just a smile.

_____

_____

_____

STRONG ON THE INSIDE

One of the servants answered, "I have seen a son of
Jesse of Bethlehem who knows how to play the lyre.
He is a brave man and a warrior. He speaks well and
is a fine-looking man. And the LORD is with him."

1 SAMUEL 16:18

David, the son of Jesse of Bethlehem, was kind of small and didn't
look strong at all. He didn't look like the typical guy you would
think of when you imagine someone who is strong and brave. But
David faced a lion, a bear, and the giant Goliath, and he was able
to defeat each one, head-on. Do you know why? It wasn't about his
size. It was because the Lord was with him. He knew that God was
watching over him and protecting him and that he had nothing to
fear because of God. And the reward for his bravery and faith was
great: The Israelite army was able to win the battle, and David's
people didn't have to live in fear anymore. David was also given
great wealth and the king's daughter's hand in marriage.

If you want to be brave like David, have faith in God. Push past
your fear, no matter how small or big it is. Raise your hand in class
to ask a question. Don't be afraid to tell your parents the truth when
you lose something. Get up and try again if you fell over the hurdle.
Know that you can face anything because the Lord is with you.

REFLECT

Imagine three good things that you could do if you had no fear of what
would happen. They can be small things (sing a solo during choir practice
or try out for a sports team) or big things (invent the next big technological
breakthrough or become a sports superstar).

USING YOUR TIME
AND ATTENTION TO WORSHIP

Jesus answered, "It is written:
'Worship the Lord your God and serve him only.'"

LUKE 4:8

Worshiping God can mean a lot of things. And no matter how you
do it, praise and worship are really important to the Lord.

But there are two things to know about worship:

1. **We worship with our time and attention.** Worship is not
   only singing praises to God. The Bible also calls "service" worship. When we give our time and attention to something, it's
   like we are worshiping it. For example, if you spend six hours
   playing a video game one day but zero minutes reading God's
   Word or talking to Him (or even thinking about Him), what do
   you think the Lord would say you worshiped that day? That's
   why, since the Bible tells us that serving others is like serving
   God, serving others can also be a form of worshiping God.

2. **Singing or speaking praises and worship is really important to God.** The next time you have an opportunity to
   worship at church or anywhere, really focus. Close your eyes
   so you're not distracted by the things around you. If you're
   singing, pay attention to the words, and sing them straight to
   Jesus. If you're speaking, say the words straight to His heart.
   The Bible says we can worship with instruments, our voices,
   and even our bodies.

REFLECT

What are some ideas you can use to worship at any time, no matter where
you are or what you're doing? Write a few down.

_____

_____

_____

SEEKING THE WISDOM OF OTHERS

Listen to advice and accept discipline,
and at the end you will be counted among the wise.

PROVERBS 19:20

All of us have people we look up to—people who, if our life turned out like theirs, we'd be thrilled. These are our role models. Some of us may even have mentors—people in our lives whom we look to for direction, instruction, and advice. Advice is really important, especially when you need help thinking through a situation. But you shouldn't take advice from just anyone. Always be looking for wise counsel.

Not all counsel (or advice) is good. Some people give poor advice that might push you toward bad decisions. But when you ask the right people for help, you will always make a wiser decision. So don't be afraid to ask people for advice. The Bible says that when you do, and when you have more than one person whom you can go to for this guidance, there is safety.

Whether it's a role model, a mentor, or just someone you look up to, know who your personal heroes are, and always be ready to ask for their input.

REFLECT

Are there people you look up to who would give you good, godly advice? Try to write down at least five of their names. The next time you need advice, ask some of these people.

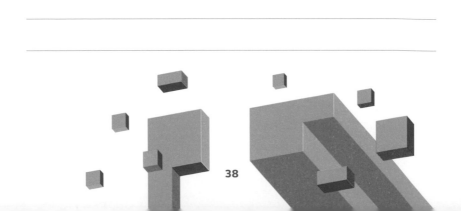

YOU'VE GOT THIS!

But seek first his kingdom and his righteousness,
and all these things will be given to you as well.

MATTHEW 6:33

You're getting older, and that means you're becoming more independent. You're beginning to make more and more of your own decisions. It's really important that you have a method for making these independent decisions and that you realize that there can be good and bad consequences for almost any decision. You can figure out which decisions will lead to good consequences and which will lead to bad ones if you focus on God's Kingdom. God's Kingdom is basically everything that has to do with God, being a Christian, and biblical principles. It's God's way of doing things, and when you read and study His Word, you become familiar with it.

The disciples had concerns about getting their needs met and knowing what decisions they should make in their everyday lives. It was easy to know what to do when Jesus was there telling them the answers. But soon, He was going to go away, and they were going to have to be more independent.

Jesus told them that if they just sought out God's way of doing things, they would have their needs met, and they wouldn't be confused about what to do. The answers would come to them. Jesus was saying, "You've got this! Just seek God." The same message applies to you today. No matter how much responsibility is on your shoulders, if you follow God's way of doing things, Jesus says, "You've got this!"

REFLECT

What are some ways you're becoming more independent? Ask a parent or guardian or older sibling to help you find a scripture in God's Word that will give you some direction. Write it down here.

_____

_____

_____

GIVE YOUR FRIENDS
THE BEST GIFT EVER

Therefore go and make disciples of all nations, baptizing them in
the name of the Father and of the Son and of the Holy Spirit,
and teaching them to obey everything I have commanded you.
And surely I am with you always, to the very end of the age.

MATTHEW 28:19–20

When we find something good, we want to tell others, so that
they can benefit, too. We want them to share in the same joy that
we have.

God's Word is one of the best gifts—better than anything that this
world can offer. It gives us hope, provides peace, inspires faith, and
reminds us of God's great love for us. The Word of God, along with
salvation and the Holy Spirit, is the best gift there is . . . and it's free!
Jesus instructs us to teach others everything that He taught the
disciples. It's normal to feel a bit nervous about sharing God's Word
with others, but many times, God will open their heart to receive
it. And they will! They might even let you say a prayer with them.
Sometimes, they need that prayer more than you realize.

How do your friends who don't know God discover that He is
real? They meet God through you. Your friends get to see God
through how you live your life and what you say or do. You are the
one whom God has selected to represent Him to your school, your
friends, and your teammates.

REFLECT

Write down the names of three friends whom you would like to share God's
Word with. Then pray and ask God to open their hearts and give you an
opportunity to speak to them about His Word.

HOW TO SAY "NO" TO SOMETHING YOU WANT

Submit yourselves, then, to God.
Resist the devil, and he will flee from you.

JAMES 4:7

"Those cookies sure do look delicious—and no one will see if I eat a few before dinner!"

"It won't hurt anyone if I go over on my video game time. No one is paying attention."

Sometimes, we are tempted to do things that we know we are not supposed to do. We make excuses, or sometimes we may even feel like the rule we're breaking is unfair. So we do things that we know we shouldn't, and we fall to temptation.

When we fall to temptation, sometimes we might hurt someone else. But we always hurt ourselves, every time. It's because when we fall, we are listening to Satan and walking away from doing as God commands.

When Satan tries to tempt you into doing wrong, the Bible says we can get him to flee if we resist him. How do you resist something? You say "No!" and go in the opposite direction. When the enemy sees your obedience to God, he will run away from you, because he knows God is on your side, and he is terrified of God. Every time you resist temptation and obey God, it gets easier, because Satan knows that messing with you is just not worth it.

REFLECT

Write down a temptation you faced recently. How did it make you feel? Why was it so tempting? And how did you feel after you resisted it?

WHY YOU'RE PERFECT

God made [Jesus] who had no sin to be sin for us, so that
in him [Jesus] we might become the righteousness of God.

2 CORINTHIANS 5:21

You may be really hard on yourself and think you have a lot of
flaws. Or maybe you're one of those people who are naturally really
confident, and you think that you're pretty awesome. When it
comes to how you should think of yourself, it's best to go back to
the One who created you and find out what He thinks of you.

In 2 Corinthians, we see that because we believe in Jesus, we are
the "righteousness of God." But what is righteousness? It means
"right-standing with God," and it has to do with how God sees you.
When God calls you righteous, it means He sees you as perfect.
This is not because you behave well, or because you don't sin. It
is ONLY because you believe Jesus is your Lord and savior! Isn't
that awesome?

Righteousness is not something we can earn. It is a free gift,
given by God's grace, that says that because you made Jesus your
Lord, God sees you just as perfectly as He sees Himself. So the next
time you're tempted to be hard on yourself, remember, you are
perfect in God's eyes.

REFLECT

Write this down on a sticky note and put it up someplace where you will see
it every day (like on your bathroom mirror): "Because of Jesus, God sees me
as '*perfect*.'" Make a point to say this at least once a day while you're getting
ready in the morning, to remind yourself how your Creator feels about you.
After doing this for a week, come back to this page and write about how
you feel.

_____

_____

_____

FORGIVING YOURSELF

If we confess our sins, he is faithful and just and will
forgive us our sins and purify us from all unrighteousness.

1 JOHN 1:9

One day, our son Joshua broke my coffeepot when he was putting
away the dishes. I was upset about it but not mad at him—my
coffeepot can be replaced. But he was so mad at himself. He felt
guilty. Because of his mistake, I couldn't make coffee. He apolo-
gized, and I let him know that he was completely forgiven. After
that, it was easier for him to forgive himself and stop feeling guilty.

Have you ever done something wrong—by mistake, or even on
purpose—and then felt guilty about it? You can ask for forgiveness
from any person you've done anything wrong to; after they give
it to you, you may find it easier to forgive yourself. You should also
know that Jesus forgives you, and He doesn't hold what you did
against you. All you have to do is ask for His forgiveness, and He
can take those bad feelings from you. Jesus doesn't want you to
feel guilty. He wants you to forgive yourself.

PRAYER

*Jesus, I ask for Your forgiveness for _____. Thank You for forgiving me.
Please help me forgive myself. In Your name I pray, amen.*

REFLECT

Forgiving yourself is much easier once you've received forgiveness from the
Lord. If you're feeling guilty, say the prayer above. Then write how you feel.

_____

_____

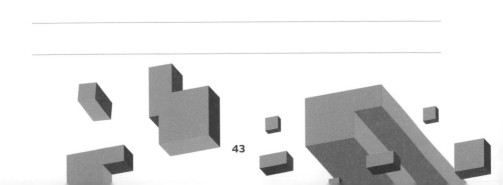

WHAT YOU SAY MATTERS

The words of the reckless pierce like swords,
but the tongue of the wise brings healing.

PROVERBS 12:18

Has anyone ever said something to you that really affected you? Perhaps it hurt your feelings or made you think bad thoughts about yourself. Or maybe it had the opposite effect—it made you feel great and empowered you to accomplish something awesome. In those moments, we realize how much what we say matters. Your words can really hurt someone, or they can make them feel fantastic.

The Bible says that we will have to answer to the Lord for every careless word we've spoken. He's watching what we say, and He really wants us to say good things. Sometimes, we don't think about it and say words God would never want us to speak. If you want to know whether what you're saying is acceptable to the Lord, ask yourself, "Would God say this?" If He absolutely would not, try to take that out of your vocabulary. As we grow, we want our voice to sound more and more like God's.

REFLECT

Can you think of some really great things people have said to you that affected you in a positive way? Write them down here, and then try to say some things like these to the people you encounter this week. See how important your words are to them.

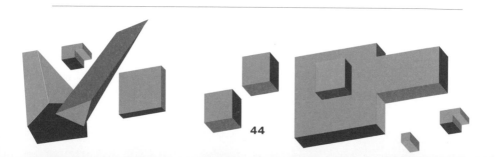

COPING WITH STRONG EMOTIONS

Like a city whose walls are broken through
is a person who lacks self-control.

PROVERBS 25:28

During biblical times, cities had walls around them to keep bad guys out and protect the city inside. If the walls ever broke down, the city was left unprotected, and anyone could get in and wreak havoc. When we aren't able to control ourselves—like when we take action while we are angry or upset—we leave ourselves totally unprotected, like those cities with no walls.

As you grow older, you may notice that you are feeling stronger emotions than you used to. Sometimes, the anger you experience feels angrier than it did when you were a kid. You may even feel a difference compared to how you felt one year ago. That's all normal—it's part of growing up. But it's really important to learn how to cope with these new, stronger emotions. The Bible says that we may get angry, but that's not an excuse for doing wrong.

If you've found yourself experiencing more intense anger and frustration, make sure to talk to a trusted adult about it. Tell them you've been dealing with some sadness or anger and want to talk through it.

REFLECT

A great exercise to get emotions under control is breathing. If you're feeling like you are about to lose it, stop. Take four deep breaths, in through your nose and out through your mouth. If doing this once doesn't make you feel more relaxed, do it again. When you breathe deeply, your body is sending signals to your brain that everything is okay. Jesus said He gave us peace, so once you are able, pray to Him and ask Him for His peace. You'll feel better in no time. Below, write about how breathing and praying felt for you.

_____

_____

_____

IT'S OKAY TO GRIEVE

The LORD is close to the brokenhearted
and saves those who are crushed in spirit.

PSALM 34:18

Sometimes in life, terrible things happen that make us feel very sad. We may lose a family member, a pet may die, or an opportunity that we'd really had our heart set on may not come through. When we experience a loss like this, it is not just okay to grieve—it's actually important for you to grieve. We should feel the feelings of loss, so that we can heal from the bad things that happened.

Even Jesus grieved. When He found out His cousin John the Baptist died, Jesus went away to be by Himself for a while. He probably wanted to think, talk to God, and maybe even cry for a bit.

The Bible says that when your heart hurts, God is right there with you. He loves you and cares about your feelings. He's close and wants you to know that, even though it may not feel like it in the moment, everything is going to be okay.

REFLECT

If you've suffered a loss and are hurting, find someone you know who loves you. Write their name down below. Tell them you're sad and want to talk about the situation, then ask if they will pray with you for Jesus to heal your heart. He will. That's exactly why He came to this earth.

_____

_____

_____

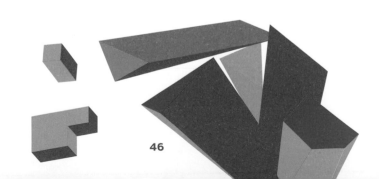

FEELING LEFT OUT

Peace I leave with you; my peace I give you.
I do not give to you as the world gives.
Do not let your hearts be troubled and do not be afraid.

JOHN 14:27

Have you ever felt like you were the only one not invited to someone's birthday party? Have you ever tried to become part of a
conversation your friends or siblings were having, only to find that
they were not that interested in what you had to say? You might
have even had your family make an important decision without
asking for your input. It can be easy to feel left out or frustrated
when these things happen. But Jesus doesn't want your heart to be
troubled. He gave you His peace.

Don't worry that your friends or family might not want your
input. A peaceful mind thinks positive thoughts about the situation. Maybe they could only have a few people at that party,
or maybe your family had to make a quick decision. Either way,
there's always another time to be involved, so you can ask Jesus for
His special kind of peace, which keeps you from thinking troubled
or fearful thoughts.

REFLECT

Think about a situation where you felt left out, and write down a positive
thought about the situation—a thought that reminds you of the peace that
comes from Jesus.

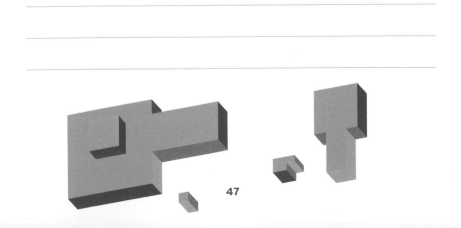

47

GOD CREATED EVERYTHING ABOUT YOU

I praise you because I am fearfully and wonderfully made;
your works are wonderful, I know that full well.

PSALM 139:14

One of the most fabulous creations that God ever made was you. When He created the earth and the universe, He spoke things into creation. But when it came to you, He had to go a different route. He got hands-on. He formed you and created you so well that He stopped making any more versions of you.

Because you are fearfully and wonderfully made, you can feel good about who you are. Whatever you see as flaws in yourself, know that they are not. Remember that God created everything about you and that everything that God makes is impressive, including you! You are a strong, original, creative, intelligent, handsome young man. You have a lot to offer people, and the world is a better place because you are in it. You are one of God's favorite creations, and He loves you, unconditionally. No matter what people say or do to you, know that you are still amazing.

REFLECT

List three things that you like most about yourself, and thank God for making you that way.

_____

_____

_____

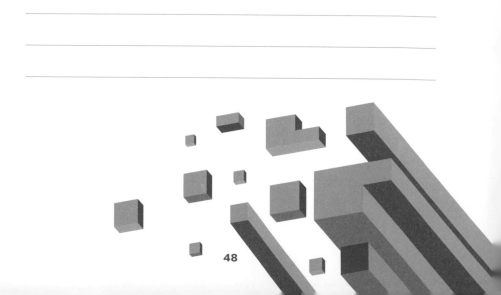

LOVING EVERY FACE AND EVERY RACE

From one man he made all the nations, that they should inhabit the whole earth; and he marked out their appointed times in history and the boundaries of their lands.

ACTS 17:26

We all come from God. He created every human being beautiful, no matter what shape or color they are. He decided who we would be, and our background is actually a part of God's plan—He decided which family you would be born into. Every race, culture, ability, and family are part of His plan, and He created us all with great and equal value. No group of people is higher or lower than another. Your beauty and worth in this world come from God, not from how the world treats you. And God loves you so much.

We are all God's children, equally beautiful in His eyes. So He commands us to love our brothers and sisters, to value who they are and where they come from, and to treat them with respect. The differences we see in one another are never excuses to mistreat them. We are all important to God. We should love everyone He has created as we love ourselves. Remember, we are all part of God's family. God makes it clear to us in His Word that if we genuinely love Him, we should love one another, too.

REFLECT

Write down some reflections about what it means to you to be equal in the eyes of God.

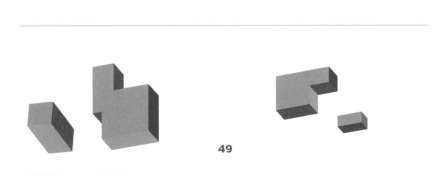

WE'LL GO FARTHER TOGETHER

Two are better than one, because they have a good return for their labor: If either of them falls down, one can help the other up. But pity anyone who falls and has no one to help them up.

ECCLESIASTES 4:9-10

An old African proverb says that if you want to go fast, go alone, but if you want to go far, go together. We can accomplish some things alone, but we can do even greater things together.

God shows us an example of teamwork through the Trinity: Father, Son, and Holy Spirit. They each have different roles, but they are one team. Just like the Trinity, we do better work when we work together.

There are five critical parts of teamwork to remember:

1. **Commitment:** Be more committed to the team than you are to getting your own way.
2. **Humility:** Decide that you don't know everything, and you need the help of others.
3. **Dependability:** Always do your part for the team, no matter how hard it gets.
4. **Flexibility:** Be able to change when needed so that the team can succeed.
5. **Selflessness:** Sacrifice for the good of the team in order to accomplish the common goal.

REFLECT

What are some other critical qualities to have as a team player? Write about why you think those qualities are essential.

_____

_____

_____

NOW IT'S YOUR TURN

Go to the ant, you sluggard; consider its ways and be wise!
It has no commander, no overseer or ruler, yet it stores
its provisions in summer and gathers its food at harvest.

PROVERBS 6:6-8

As you grow, you will find that your parents expect more from you
and give you more responsibilities around the house. As you get
used to your responsibilities, you might want to think about ants.
Ants are always responsible, without ever having to be told what to
do. They just do their work. Your parents will expect you to do your
chores without being told, just like the ant. If you have practice or
lessons, you will be expected to keep track of your own schedule.

As you take on more responsibility, you are exercising the
"muscles" you need to grow into a successful adult. Expect to take
responsibility for your actions, because you are your own person.
And as you grow into your own person, you should not blame
others for your decisions, reactions, or when you forget something.

To be responsible, you must have good habits. Write down
important stuff, such as homework assignments and meeting
dates and times. Check the time regularly, so you are never late.
Ask questions when you don't understand. Clean up after yourself
when you make a mess. Check in with your parents, so they know
where you are. Keep a calendar of your lessons, practices, games,
and meetings. As you do this, you will become more and more
responsible for your own actions and self, just like the ant.

REFLECT

List some other ways that you can be more responsible around the house.

_____

_____

_____

GOOD SECRETS AND BAD SECRETS

A gossip betrays a confidence, but a trustworthy person
keeps a secret . . . but victory is won through many advisers.

PROVERBS 11:13–14

It's good to have trustworthy friends and also to be a trusted friend.
Because they trust you, your friends may tell you secrets they think
you'll keep safe and not share with others. When you tell those
secrets to others, it can make your friends feel bad or embarrassed.
It also makes you seem like a bad friend.

There are good secrets and bad secrets. Good secrets are safe
and harmless, like a crush, a bad grade on a test, or an embarrass-
ing restroom accident. Keeping those secrets is part of being a
good friend. Bad secrets are those that are dangerous or harmful to
people. If a friend tells you a secret that you think might be dangerous for them or others, you should seek God's guidance and tell a
parent or trusted adult. Your friend's safety is even more important
than keeping their secrets.

As you get older, you may see or hear things that you think you
can't tell your parents about because you'll get in trouble. This will
tempt you to keep them a secret. But you should bring these things
to your parents or guardians—God put them in your life to help
you. King Solomon, whom the Bible calls one of the wisest men to
ever live, tells us that there is safety when we seek wise counsel. So
always keep open lines of communication with trusted adults and
with God.

REFLECT

Can you think of a time when you told an adult a secret and helped the situation? Is there anything that you are dealing with now that you need to tell a
trusted adult?

_____

_____

_____

DON'T GIVE UP

Consider it pure joy, my brothers and sisters, whenever you face trials of many kinds, because you know that the testing of your faith produces perseverance. Let perseverance finish its work so that you may be mature and complete, not lacking anything.

JAMES 1:2-4

Our kids love making homemade cookies. After adding the ingredients and mixing the batter, they put the dough into the hot oven, and it rises. Though the dough contains all the ingredients of a cookie, the dough doesn't become a cookie until it bakes in the oven.

God uses troubles the same way that we use the oven for that cookie dough—to grow us and complete us. When you face difficult challenges, they can make you want to quit. But it's the hard times that help us grow and become more loving, faithful, and strong. James wrote that we should count it all joy when tested by hard times, because we grow into the person whom God wants us to become. Becoming better is excellent, but it takes hard work. Whether it's enduring problems in school, in friendships, or at home, God's message is the same—don't give up.

You may not understand why some challenges come your way, but just know that God is going to help you through it. God never gives up on you, and you shouldn't give up on yourself. Something beautiful will come from this, and the victory will taste even better than homemade cookies.

REFLECT

Think about something difficult that you are going through right now. Jot down a few good things that could come out of this situation.

_____

_____

_____

GROWING TOGETHER AS FRIENDS

The righteous choose their friends carefully,
but the way of the wicked leads them astray.

PROVERBS 12:26

Friends are the people in your life whom you can count on to be there for you when you need them. They are the people you enjoy hanging out and discovering life with. The best friendships are those where both you and your friend value each other and help each other grow. Friendships help you discover how to be more loving and patient. Together, you and your friends can help each other grow in character, love, and selflessness. God instructs us to choose our friends carefully, because friends can influence what we do and think. He wants you to have friends based on the life He wants you to live—a life of faith, love, and purity.

Because friends can help each other grow, we should never take them for granted. Be patient with them. Exercise kindness. Explore new things with them. Encourage each other when one of you encounters a challenge. Be the kind of friend that you would like as a friend. We should value relationships not only because we love others, but also because they allow us to grow.

REFLECT

Make a list of all the qualities that make up a good friend. Make it your goal to be that kind of friend to someone else.

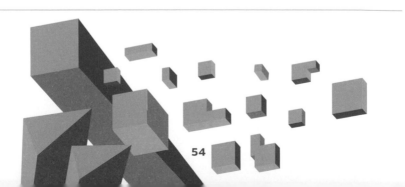

54

BEING A MAN OF YOUR WORD

When a man makes a vow to the LORD or takes an oath
to obligate himself by a pledge, he must not break his
word but must do everything he said.

NUMBERS 30:2

You grow into a godly man by being a man of your word. Think
about all the times you trusted that people would keep their word
to you. Maybe it was a teacher who said that your class would get
a special reward next week, or a promise from your parent to take
you out for ice cream tomorrow. When they made you a promise,
they were giving you their word that they would do what they said.
Every time they give you their word and follow through on the
promise, it builds trust.

God shows us the ultimate example of keeping your word, because
He honors every promise that He has ever made. We can trust God
because we know He is bound to what He says. We, as His children,
are to imitate Him. When we keep our word, we show others that we
can be trusted. Parents, friends, and teachers can trust that you will
do what you say. Keeping your word means that you are faithful and
are worthy of being respected. If you want to be a man of your word,
you must keep your word, keep your promises, and do what you say,
every time.

REFLECT

Think of a person whom you trust a lot. Why do you trust them the way you
do? Do you trust them more because they keep their promises?

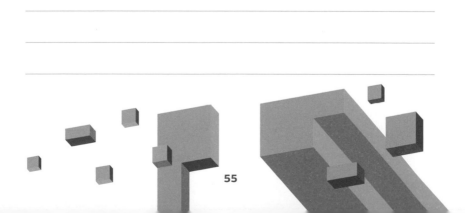

THE POWER INSIDE OF YOU

But he said to me, "My grace is sufficient for you,
for my power is made perfect in weakness." Therefore I will
boast all the more gladly about my weaknesses,
so that Christ's power may rest on me.

2 CORINTHIANS 12:9

Do you remember the story of when David fought against the giant Goliath? Or when the three Hebrew boys were put into the fiery furnace because they would not bow down to King Nebuchadnezzar? How about when Peter got out of the boat and walked on water? Or when Jesus went to the cross and died for our sins? We might think, "How could they do such extraordinary things?" But the answer is simple: God empowered them to do the miraculous, that's how.

After Jesus died and resurrected, He sent the Holy Spirit to dwell with us and in us. This Holy Spirit gave us the power to do what we could not normally do in our own strength. That's what empowerment is—strength and ability to do something special that you could not do before. The Apostle Paul lets us know that God's grace, or His empowerment, is more than enough for us to achieve victory in every situation.

Sometimes we can feel weak, but God promises that when we submit to Him, He will turn our weakness into His strength. A strength that makes the things that you thought were impossible possible.

REFLECT

List a few areas of weakness that you can submit to the Lord to receive His strength. Pray to the Holy Spirit to empower you in these areas.

_____

_____

_____

WHAT TO DO
WHEN IT GETS REALLY HARD

Let us not become weary in doing good, for at the proper time
we will reap a harvest if we do not give up.

GALATIANS 6:9

You will face tough times in life, no matter who you are. When
things get tough, it's your determination that makes the difference. If you give up every time things get hard, you will get used
to avoiding challenging situations, and it won't be easy for you to
succeed. Don't give up, no matter how hard things get.

The Apostle Paul encourages young Christians not to give up on
their faith, even in times of hardship. God uses the hard things we
go through to make us stronger. When we push through, we grow
in strength. We also grow in faith when we have to trust God. In
difficult moments, we can't always see what God is doing, but we
know He's preparing something good. Trust that what He is doing
will be good for us. This trust gives us the confidence and strength
to look to the future, instead of focusing on the current difficulties.

So how do you persevere? First, decide in your mind that quitting is not an option. Second, ask God for strength and wisdom.
Third, find a trusted adult or good friend who can encourage you.
Fourth, imagine all the good things that can happen as a result of
this. Last, expect things to change. Remember, tough times don't
last, but tough people do!

REFLECT

Think about a time when things were hard but you didn't give up. Write
down anything good that you think came from your perseverance. For example, did you learn that you can work faster than you thought you could, or
did you find new ways to make friends?

WHEN IT FEELS LIKE NO ONE WANTS YOU

The stone the builders rejected has become the cornerstone.

PSALM 118:22

You may feel rejection when someone you feel should care about you or like you—or someone you want to care about you and like you—seems like they don't. Perhaps you felt rejected when you didn't get picked for a team, or when a parent left the family. Maybe you felt rejected when you felt like no one liked you and there was nothing you could do about it.

Jesus knew exactly what it feels like to be rejected. The stone that the writer is talking about in this psalm is actually Jesus. He was rejected by His own people but then became the most important "stone" of them all—the cornerstone. He was the stone on which God built His house. Jesus also knew that God would never leave Him, so even though He felt rejection, He was never afraid or discouraged.

If you're feeling rejected, remember that Jesus came to love you and to heal your broken heart, and He will never, ever leave you. So do not be afraid or discouraged. No matter how others feel about you or treat you, Jesus loves you and thinks you are awesome.

REFLECT

Are you feeling rejected? Write down a prayer asking for healing, and take time to reflect on Jesus's love for you.

_____

_____

_____

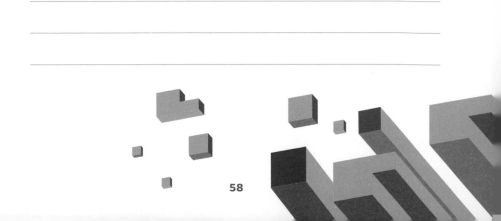

DOING YOUR PART

And do not forget to do good and to share with others,
for with such sacrifices God is pleased.

HEBREWS 13:16

You may have a big family with lots of siblings or a small family where it's just you and Mom, but the message is the same: Love your family. And show that love, through your actions and your words. A great way to show your family that you care is by doing your part around the house.

Doing your part could mean doing chores, going to get the mail, or helping prepare dinner with Mom or Dad. It's anything that adds to the well-being of others. When we are good to our family, it makes God smile. He knows that it can be a sacrifice to do the dishes when you want to play outside with your friends. But your sacrifice honors God and shows that you want the best for your family.

Another kind of sacrifice is sharing. When you share, you show your family that it is more important to give than it is to keep things for yourself. God loves when we share. God is a big giver, so when we share, we are acting just like Him.

REFLECT

Parents really enjoy it when you do your part. List three ways that you can help out around the house this week. See whether you can do it before a parent or guardian asks you to. It will put a smile on their face.

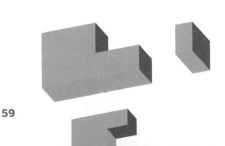

HUMILITY, THEN SUCCESS

Humility is the fear of the LORD;
its wages are riches and honor and life.

PROVERBS 22:4

It's easy to think that you know everything or know what to do in any situation. And it may seem that all the smart, popular, or happy people know everything and can do everything by themselves. But the secret is that successful people don't do it all on their own. They are always trying to listen and learn, and they ask for help when they need it.

When you are on a sports team, it takes humility to listen to the coaches. At school, it takes humility to ask for help. At home, it takes humility to admit when you are wrong. And in all aspects of life, it takes humility to listen and live as God commands.

Sometimes, it's easy to listen and ask for help. Other times, it can be hard, especially when it hurts our pride. But when we practice humility, God promises success and a close relationship with Him.

REFLECT

To exercise humility, practice listening. Focus on understanding what others are saying and how they are feeling. Try not to interrupt. See whether your friends and family notice a difference. Write down how it feels to listen this way.

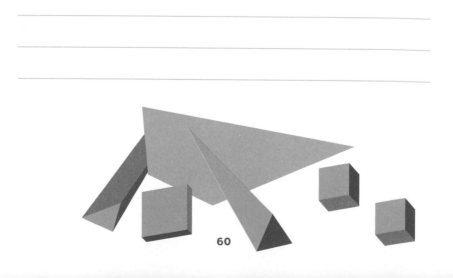

WHEN THE CHOICE IS HARD TO MAKE

Enter through the narrow gate. For wide is the gate and broad is
the road that leads to destruction, and many enter through it.
But small is the gate and narrow the road that leads to life,
and only a few find it.

MATTHEW 7:13-14

Some choices are pretty easy to make, like when you need to decide
whether you want chocolate or vanilla ice cream. When the choice
is just a matter of opinion and there is no right or wrong answer
(like with ice cream), it's okay to choose whatever sounds best to
you. But sometimes, the choice is much more difficult to make.
Sometimes, you have to choose between doing the wrong thing or
the right thing. This is when you must choose the narrow "gate."

The wide gate is usually the way that most people go. They
choose the route that seems the easiest or the most fun or is what
everyone else is doing. But just because it's easy doesn't mean that
it's the right choice. What if everyone else is making fun of another
person and you decide to join them? That would be the wrong
choice. When you have a difficult decision to make, the broad way
might seem easiest, but it will lead to problems and "destruction."
Choosing to enter through the narrow gate may seem more difficult and less popular, but as the scripture says, it leads to life and
blessings. Be one of the few who find it.

REFLECT

Is there a difficult choice that you're facing right now or that you've recently
faced? Write it down here, then discuss it with someone you look up to.
Talk about which choice might be the broad way and which might be the
narrow gate.

DON'T WORRY, BE JOYFUL!

You make known to me the path of life; you will fill me with joy in your presence, with eternal pleasures at your right hand.

PSALM 16:11

Life is filled with twists and turns, ups and downs. One week might be great, and the next week might be difficult. It can be hard to find joy when things are not going well. But you don't have to let your worries or bad feelings bring you down. You can find comfort, joy, and happiness in any situation with God.

Joy is a fruit of the spirit. It's the attitude that God has. When we love Him and serve Him, it brings Him great joy. I know that every time my daughter is around puppies, it brings her great joy. The good news is that we all can get that same kind of joy from just being in God's presence. Spending time with God is one of the greatest ways that we can receive joy in our hearts.

When we pray and talk to God just like we'd talk to a friend, it will always leave us feeling much better. Spending time with God is what we need to turn a bad week into a good week, and a good week into a great week.

REFLECT

Take a moment to pray to God today. Thank Him for His blessings. Write down your worries and struggles, and ask Him to help you with them. Allow Him to fill your heart with joy.

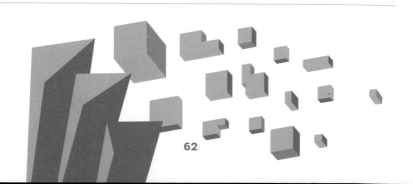

IF LOVE WAS CLOTHING

Therefore, as God's chosen people, holy and dearly loved,
clothe yourselves with compassion, kindness, humility,
gentleness and patience.

COLOSSIANS 3:12

Every time we are kind to people, we allow others to have an
encounter with God. Kindness is a fruit of the spirit, which means
it originates from God. Some people see kindness as a weakness,
because it can take shape in gentle words, forgiveness for those
who wronged you, or giving more than you take. But kindness
is not weakness—it's a gentle strength, strength that comes from
a powerful God. Being kind is how we show others the love and
strength of God.

You can show kindness by giving up your seat in the lunchroom
when there aren't any more seats left. Or by sharing the last piece
of cake with your sibling, even though they wouldn't share their
stuff with you earlier. God knows it's not easy to be kind, especially when you are having a bad day or someone is being mean
to you. Just as He provides for everything else that is good in our
lives, God provides us the strength to show kindness. Ask for God's
help today.

PRAYER

*Father, help me be strong and clothed in kindness, just like You.
Show others who You are through my kindness. In Jesus's name, amen.*

REFLECT

Think about a time you were kind to someone. How did it make you feel?
How do you think it made the other person(s) feel?

_____

_____

_____

DOING YOUR BEST

Whatever your hand finds to do, do it with all your might . . .

ECCLESIASTES 9:10A

Statistics show that Japanese children usually score higher than American children on standardized math tests. A study involving first graders was done to find out why. In the study, the children were asked to solve a hard puzzle—the researchers were not watching to see whether they could solve the puzzle, but how long the children would work on it before giving up. On average, the American children lasted 9.47 minutes. The Japanese children lasted 13.93 minutes. This means that the Japanese children tried about 40 percent longer. Researchers concluded that the difference in math scores had less to do with how smart the kids were and more to do with how hard they tried.

Many times in life, we might think that others are just naturally smarter, stronger, or better than we are. But they just decide to try harder. God wants us to try hard and give it our best in anything that we do. Trying our best gives us the opportunity to see God's best, all the great things that God has placed inside of us. You may not know what you can do until you push yourself to be the best that you can be. If you're going to soccer practice, train with all your might. If you're serving others, go the extra mile. You can always be proud when you have given your best effort. Like a good father, God is always pleased when we try with all of our might. It's how we give Him glory.

REFLECT

What's the hardest thing that you can remember doing? Once it was over, did you feel proud of yourself for giving your best effort?

_____

_____

_____

RESPECTING THOSE IN CHARGE

Let everyone be subject to the governing authorities, for
there is no authority except that which God has established.
The authorities that exist have been established by God.

ROMANS 13:1

Your parents, guardians, teachers, and pastors/ministry leaders
are examples of authority figures whom God placed in your life to
help, guide, and correct you. When you understand and trust that
these authority figures want what's best for you, you will be able to
obey them, honor them, and show them respect, even when you
don't enjoy what they are doing. For example, it may not always
feel good to have your parents discipline you if you lie, but they are
trying to teach you an important lesson about honesty.

The authority figures in your life may not always be perfect, but
you should always respect them. When you don't show respect,
you are rebelling against what God has set in place. When you do
that, you leave yourself open to bad situations.

Respecting those in charge means valuing their instruction
and listening to their direction. Some things you can do to respect
those in charge are to speak politely to them, do what they ask you
to do quickly, be attentive to them, and always listen whenever
they speak.

REFLECT

How well do you think that you show respect? Has someone in charge ever
thanked you for showing respect to them?

_____

_____

_____

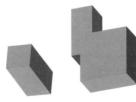

THE REAL POINT OF SCHOOL

... for giving prudence to those who are simple, knowledge
and discretion to the young—let the wise listen and
add to their learning, and let the discerning get guidance.

PROVERBS 1:4–5

You are not alone if you have ever wondered, "What's the point of
school?" Many students have pondered the same question. It can
be hard to do your best in school when you don't understand why
it's important or maybe even are struggling to understand some of
the things you are being taught.

But school doesn't exist just so you can have somewhere to go
while your parents are at work. The goal of school is to help you
grow into a well-rounded adult and teach you discipline, character,
and perseverance. Education isn't just about the information being
taught; it is also meant to help you discover the great things inside
of you. Long ago, children were taught to read mainly so that they
could read the Bible and learn the Word of God. The Bible was actually a textbook in schools back then.

God tells us that it is wise to continue to learn. If school seems
challenging sometimes, that's because it's meant to be, to help
you grow. God uses school to help you get better. Even if you don't
understand the assignment or don't feel like doing the homework,
remember that God is using it to help you grow.

REFLECT

List three ways besides learning about a subject that school can help you
become a better person. Do you think those are traits that can help you be
successful in life?

WATCH WHAT YOU SAY

The tongue has the power of life and death,
and those who love it will eat its fruit.

PROVERBS 18:21

There was once a scientist who performed an experiment on rice with a classroom of children. He put cooked rice in three separate jars. On one jar, he wrote "thank you." On the next jar, he wrote "you fool." And on the third jar, he wrote nothing at all. He then instructed the children to say what was on the labels, out loud, every day, to each jar of rice. The children listened, thanking the first jar, insulting the second jar, and ignoring the third jar.

After 30 days, the rice in the jar labeled "thank you" had hardly changed and had begun to ferment, giving off a sweet smell. The jar labeled "you fool" was moldy, rotten, and stinky. The jar that was ignored had a small amount of mold in it. Even though the rice didn't have brains or ears, the words still affected it.

This experiment demonstrates something that God shows us many times in His Word: Your words have power. Words can create and change things. Words can make others feel good, or they can make others feel bad. Words have the power to change how you see situations. Words are an important power that God has given you, and you must use them wisely.

REFLECT

Here's a challenge for you: For the next five days, try really hard to only say positive words. When you would normally complain, find something positive to say. At the end of the five days, come back to this page and write down what happened.

_____

_____

_____

WHEN IT'S JUST TAKING TOO LONG

The end of a matter is better than its beginning,
and patience is better than pride.

ECCLESIASTES 7:8

We took a family trip to Disney World a few years ago, and the lines for the rides were *so* long. We had to wait for hours! Waiting like that can feel frustrating, because no one likes to wait. We would all like to have everything that we want right now, but that's not possible. As we grow up, we learn that patience is necessary.

Patience is listed in the Bible as one of the fruits of the spirit. That means it's the attitude that God has, and we are supposed to copy it. To be patient means to be at peace while waiting. When we learn to wait, not only do we become patient with the world—we also become more patient with God. We grow our ability to wait for His plan to unfold.

Here is a plan to help you become more patient. The first thing you should always do is ask God for His help in growing your ability to wait. Next, ask yourself, "Will anything bad happen to me by waiting?" (The answer is probably "no.") Last, while you are waiting, fix your focus on something else. It always helps time go by faster if you can distract yourself with something fun or constructive. No one looks forward to being patient, but you can decide to have a good attitude while you wait.

REFLECT

What are some constructive things that you can do while you wait? Write them out, so you have everything you need to do the things you thought of.

_____

_____

_____

BUILDING CHARACTER

The LORD God took the man and put him in the
Garden of Eden to work it and take care of it.

GENESIS 2:15

When I was growing up, I had a lot of chores to do around the
house. I would have to clean the bathrooms, wash the floors, wash
the dishes, vacuum, and mow our grass—plus our neighbor's grass,
too! I felt like there was always something to do around the house,
and I was always the guy to do it. I would ask my mom, "Why do I
have to do all this work?" Her reply was always the same: "It's build-
ing character, David." What did this mean? It meant that she was
teaching me the value of working hard so I could do well in life.

Almost all great things in life come at a cost. The cost is the effort
that we are willing to put into them. God promises that the effort that
we give will not be for nothing, that we will receive a benefit. Even
the things that God wants us to do will require some hard work at
times. Hard work and strong faith are how we accomplish God's will.

There is a saying, "Hard work beats talent when talent fails to
work hard." It's impossible to be successful in school, at a job, on a
team, or in relationships without hard work. If you pay the cost of
hard work, you will be able to achieve your dreams.

REFLECT

Write down two things you can work harder at. Ask God to give you the
strength to work hard at anything you set your mind or hands to.

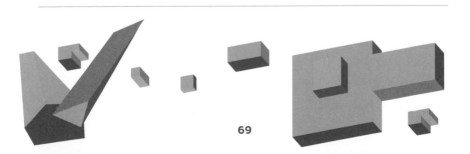

UNITED TOGETHER AS ONE FAMILY

Both the one who makes people holy and those who are
made holy are of the same family. So Jesus is not
ashamed to call them brothers and sisters.

HEBREWS 2:11

We all come from different backgrounds. You might sit across the
lunch table from someone who is eating a food from their culture that you've never seen before. You might have a friend who
sounds different from you when they talk because their family is
from a different country. Every day, you can find differences about
others that stand out. But we shouldn't hide or ever be ashamed of
our differences. We should celebrate those differences. As we do, it
brings us closer together. As Christians, we are all God's children,
which means we are all spiritually connected. That makes us
spiritual brothers and sisters with others who have received Jesus
as their savior.

Even though we come from different families, cultures, and
backgrounds, we can all claim God as our father—our spiritual
father. As a great father, He wants us to get along with one another
and love one another. Love is what unifies us. We can still be proud
of our differences. But we should never let those differences divide
us or get in the way of friendship, community, and serving God
together. We now have the same family. Jesus is not ashamed to
call us brothers and sisters, and we shouldn't be, either.

REFLECT

Differences can sometimes make others feel embarrassed or left out. Write
down some ways that you can make others feel good about their differences
when they are around you.

_____

_____

_____

GOD KEEPS HIS PROMISES

Know therefore that the LORD your God is God; he is the faithful
God, keeping his covenant of love to a thousand generations
of those who love him and keep his commandments.

DEUTERONOMY 7:9

Have you ever had a friend or a sibling who broke a promise? It can
be a real bummer when someone we trust doesn't do what they
said they would do. Sometimes it can cause us to wonder whether
others will treat us the same way. God, however, is not like that. He
always keeps His promises.

A covenant is like the ultimate promise. In the Scriptures, when
someone would make a covenant agreement, they would keep
that covenant even if it hurt them. It's the greatest show of faithfulness. When God talks about keeping His Covenant, He's talking
about His promises. Did you know that the Bible is filled with over
7,000 promises to us as His children? You can always trust God,
because He keeps every promise that He makes.

Remember, God is not like your friends, peers, or others. He
cannot lie. That means that what He says is guaranteed. He promises us peace, healing, love, joy, wisdom, and more. You can have
faith in God and trust Him to come through, every time.

REFLECT

Think of three things that are going on in your life, or areas of your heart,
in which you need to trust God to come through on His promise. Write
them below, then consider talking with a trusted adult about them and
praying together.

_____

_____

_____

PRESS PAUSE

My dear brothers and sisters, take note of this: Everyone should be quick to listen, slow to speak and slow to become angry.

JAMES 1:19

Have you ever said something in anger, then felt bad about it? Or seen someone speak when angry and then regret what they said? Sometimes, when we are angry, it's difficult to move slowly and think about what we really want to say, but there is always a benefit to being slow to speak. God's Word tells us to stop and listen before we respond to someone. Then, when you're ready to say something back, "press pause" and ask yourself, "Is this really what I should say right now?" We should all stop before we "talk back" or act rashly and ask ourselves, "Will something good come out of this or something bad? Am I reflecting God with this action?"

Don't speak up and argue out of frustration or anger. When you do, the words almost never come out right. Instead, press pause, count to ten, and make sure that you've listened to everything the other person has to say and that you are not about to say something you'll regret. Who knows? If you do what God's Word tells you, you may be the person who solves the problem!

REFLECT

Tell your parent or guardian that you are practicing being "slow to speak and slow to anger," and you'd like them to practice with you. Come up with a realistic scenario. For example, they won't let you watch TV or play video games. Instead of arguing, ask them another question so you can practice being "quick to listen." Then, after you've pressed pause and thought about the best way to respond, say your piece. Write down what you learned below.

JUST SAY NOTHING

A gossip betrays a confidence,
but a trustworthy person keeps a secret.

PROVERBS 11:13

Sometimes, people make up hurtful stories and lies about others, and they gossip about them. But did you know that even when the stories are true, it is still gossip to repeat them? And gossip can really hurt someone else. Talking badly about someone when they are not around, whether it's true or untrue, is gossip and very damaging to them—and to your relationship.

When someone tells you something private and then you tell other people, it breaks the trust between you two. They won't want to share their secrets with you anymore. It may be a really juicy secret, and you may really want to tell others, but you must ask yourself, "Do I want to be a gossip, or do I want to be trustworthy?" It's usually better to just say nothing at all.

Important note: If you have a friend with a dangerous secret, or you're concerned that they (or someone else) will get hurt, it is best to tell a trusted adult, like a parent, guardian, teacher, or counselor. Many people have been saved from pain, abuse, or danger because someone told their secret to the right person. This is the only time when it's good to tell someone's secret.

REFLECT

Are you someone who has a hard time keeping yourself from talking negatively about others? Jot down a little prayer below asking God to help you only say positive things about others and *just say nothing* when you want to say something bad about them.

WHAT REALLY COUNTS

Keep your lives free from the love of money and be
content with what you have, because God has said,
"Never will I leave you; never will I forsake you."

HEBREWS 13:5

In your life, you have *material* things like your home, car, clothes, electronics, and even money. Then, you have *immaterial* things, like family, love, happiness, peace, your health, and spirituality. God wants you to remember that the immaterial things in your life, like His love, are so much more important than the material things.

We *do* need some material things in our lives. But instead of always wanting more, God wants us to be grateful for what we have. Sometimes, we can lose sight of what is important when we just want what other people have—the latest phone, the most advanced gaming console, or the newest shoes. It's okay to want things. But we must stay mindful of what's truly important in our lives. Instead of complaining about what you don't have, God wants you to be grateful for everything you do have, like His love and the love of friends and family.

Every day is a gift. Being healthy is a gift. Having a home and a family filled with people who love you and take care of you is a gift. All of God's blessings are gifts. Even if you don't have everything you want, remember all the great gifts that you *do* have.

REFLECT

Write one material thing that you would like. Now list three immaterial things that you are thankful for. How do each of those things make you feel?

_____

_____

_____

MAINTAINING YOUR TEMPLE

Do you not know that your bodies are temples of the Holy Spirit,
who is in you, whom you have received from God?
You are not your own.

1 CORINTHIANS 6:19

God created your body to work well—*if* you treat it right. Your body is the house where the Holy Spirit lives, and you have to treat the Holy Spirit's home with respect. In fact, your body is called a temple. A temple is a sacred place, which means you must behave a certain way there.

When you choose to treat your body well, by eating right, getting enough rest, and avoiding putting bad things (like drugs, cigarettes/vaping, and alcohol) into it, it will work well. When you treat it poorly, by eating junk foods, not getting enough sleep, or not exercising, your body will stop functioning the way it should. It's important that you take good care of your body, because it's the only one you have. Eat healthy meals, get plenty of sleep, exercise regularly, and drink plenty of water. If you take care of your body, it will work the right way and accomplish its goal, allowing you to live a long and happy life.

REFLECT

Think about how you treat your body—what you eat, your sleeping habits, and whether you exercise. On a scale of 1 to 10 (10 being amazing), how well do you think you treat your body? Write down what you can change to do better.

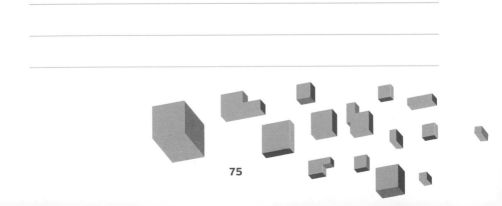

BEST FRIENDS ARE BETTER
THAN MORE FRIENDS

One who has unreliable friends soon comes to ruin,
but there is a friend who sticks closer than a brother.

PROVERBS 18:24

It can be tempting to think you need to have a lot of friends in your life. But being popular can also be pretty stressful. The pressure of trying to please so many people can make you feel like you have to act like someone you're not. But the fact is, you should feel free to be yourself. God's Word tells us that a close friend or two is much more valuable than a crowd of friends who don't care that much about you.

If people are friends with you because of what you look like or because you "fit in" to what *they* think is cool, then they don't really know you. So as soon as you have an off day, they may not want to be your friend anymore. But there is a friend out there who will stick closer to you than a brother, one who likes you for being yourself. And you don't need tons of these friends to feel happy. For true friends, quality is more important than quantity.

In the Bible, Ecclesiastes says that "two are better than one," because "if either of them falls down, one can help the other up" (4:9a, 10). It also tells us that alone, you can be overpowered, but a good friend will come to your defense (4:12). Do you want friends who will laugh at you when you fall, or ones who will help you up?

REFLECT

Do you have a close friend or two who you feel would stick with you no matter what? Write their name(s) down here and take a moment this week to thank them for being such a great friend!

_____

_____

_____

HOW TO GET BLESSED

If you love me, keep my commands.

JOHN 14:15

When Jesus came to the earth as God's only son, he had to show His love to His father. He did this by obeying and doing what God asked of Him. God sent Jesus here to do some difficult things—to forgive and save others from their sin. God did this out of love, and Jesus had to do what was asked of Him out of love for God and people.

Jesus was the greatest example of love and obedience we will ever know of, and in the Bible, Jesus Himself asks us to obey. He tells us that keeping His commands is the way to show our love for Him. Do you love Jesus? You can prove it by doing what He asks of you.

The biggest command Jesus asks us to obey in the Bible is to love one another as He loved us (John 15:12). If we can obey this, we will obey God the way Jesus did when He sacrificed His whole life out of love for us. Does this sound hard? It is. But Jesus told us that we can do anything He did, and even greater works than that, so we know that we can do it (John 14:12).

REFLECT

Are there some things God has put on your heart that you could do better in obeying Him? Write them below, and really work on them this week—out of love for Him. If you're not sure, ask a parent or guardian how they think you could obey Jesus better. Write down what you came up with together.

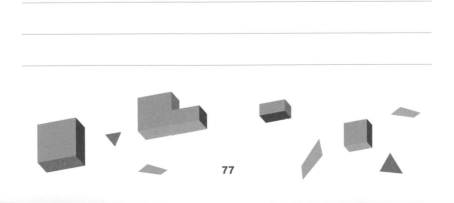

77

GODLY GOALS

I press on toward the goal to win the prize for which
God has called me heavenward in Christ Jesus.

PHILIPPIANS 3:14

Goals are the things we want to accomplish in life. You may have short-term goals that you want to get done right away, like reading one book per week, helping your parents out every day, or talking to God every day. Or maybe you have long-term goals that might not happen for many years, like getting into a good college, becoming a professional athlete, learning how to animate, or starting a business. No matter when they are for, these goals should affect how you live your life each day.

God has goals for your life. There are things He wants you to do very soon and things He wants for you in the future. When you set goals, make sure to ask God for His input, then write them down. When you write your goals down, they are much more likely to come to pass in your life.

REFLECT

If you don't have goals yet, now is a good time to set some! First, ask God, "What do you want me to do, Lord?" Then write down what comes to your heart and mind. What is a good first step you can take toward your goals?

_____

_____

_____

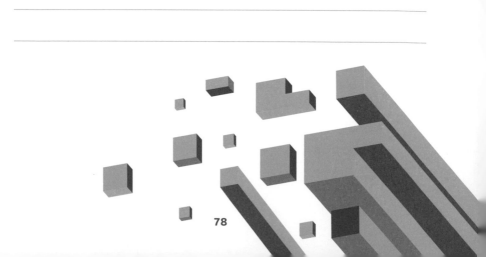

WHEN YOU DOUBT

... the one who doubts is like a wave of the sea,
blown and tossed by the wind.

JAMES 1:6B

We all experience doubt from time to time. Sometimes, you decide something, or you believe something, and then you say to yourself, "Well, maybe that isn't really true." Or "What if I'm not able to complete that project/reach that accomplishment?" Doubt may come, but when you're not really sure about something that you know you should be sure about, you should doubt your doubt.

For example, if you want to try out for the soccer team, you may start thinking, "I'm probably not good enough." Don't accept that doubtful thought that comes your way. Reject it, and instead say "Yes!" to what God says about you and your situation. He says you are victorious—because of Jesus, you've already won.

God says you should doubt any thoughts that oppose what He says. This is especially important when it comes to thoughts about God and how He feels about you. If you ever doubt God or Jesus, or doubt your salvation in Christ, reject those thoughts. Say no to Satan, and remember who God is and what He says about you: You are loved, and you are saved because of Christ. That's a thought you never need to doubt.

REFLECT

Have you recently had a thought about yourself that you know is not what God's Word says about you ("I'm stupid, I'm bad, I can't do it . . .")? Write it down here, then cross a big, dark line through it. Under it, write what God says about you instead. Need help with this? Ask an adult who loves you to help you find God's Word about your situation.

BEING A GOOD GATEKEEPER

Above all else, guard your heart,
for everything you do flows from it.

PROVERBS 4:23

The Bible speaks about the importance of the heart. Everything you do comes from it—all of your actions, thoughts, and feelings. And because of that, it is necessary to guard what goes into it.

You have gates that are like entryways to your heart: your ears, your eyes, and even your mouth. What you hear, see, and say, especially about yourself, is really important to the condition of your heart. You can open these gates to allow stuff into your heart, or you can close them when you think it's not safe—when you know something should not be allowed in.

Media like TV, music, the internet, video games, and books can be used by God to help you, but the enemy can also use these things to hurt you. The devil wants to mess with your heart so you can make bad decisions and feel badly. Ask yourself which media the devil might be trying to use to hurt you, and slam that gate closed. Say "No!" to listening to or looking at those things anymore. This way, you can guard and protect your heart.

REFLECT

Sit down with a trusted adult and talk about the media you watch, read, play, and listen to. Together, decide which ones you think are good for your heart and which ones might be bad. Write down the two lists. What will you do next?

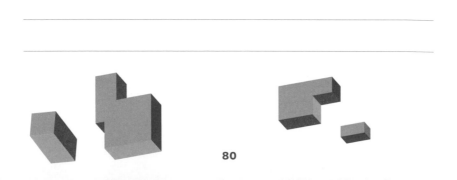

YOUR FIRST LOVE

Jesus replied: "Love the Lord your God with all your heart
and with all your soul and with all your mind."

MATTHEW 22:37

It's okay and normal to like someone and to want them to like you back. It can be exciting to feel butterflies in your stomach when they're around and intense emotions when you think about them. Sometimes, you will have a crush on someone one week but be over them the next. But other times, these feelings for someone can get so intense that they can distract you from the most important relationship: your relationship with God.

Jesus reminds us that we are to love God with all of our heart and mind. When you focus too much on a crush, you forget the most important love in your life—your love for God. When you have a crush, many times pressure from friends or the influence of music and media can make you feel like you have to take it to the next level, date them, or do something romantic. God wants us to focus on our relationship with Him first.

So what should you do about your crush? Just enjoy having them in your life! Focus on being a good friend to them. Be someone who cares about them, like you would want someone to care about you. Be a reflection of God's love in all your relationships.

REFLECT

Take some time each day to think of what God's love means to you and how you can reflect that love to others. Jot down some of the ways Jesus has taught you to show love.

_____

_____

_____

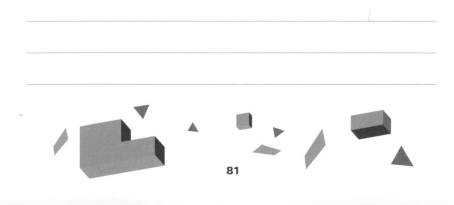

DON'T BELIEVE THE HYPE

Follow God's example, therefore, as dearly loved children.

EPHESIANS 5:1

A celebrity is usually someone who is well-known and celebrated in society, whom many people want to imitate or be like. We look to them as examples of the best thing to do. But a famous person can be hot one month and forgotten about the next. They can do something wrong and not live up to our expectations of them. And when celebrities fail, we can feel disappointed. Even though we can learn from their lives, we don't always want to follow their example—especially if they are doing or saying the wrong things.

There is one person in our life, however, who will never disappoint us—God. His love, words, and actions are everlasting. So in God we can always trust, and it is Him we should try to imitate. Why? Because we know that He will always show us the best possible example. Jesus actually did that very same thing here on earth. He imitated God just like the Bible tells us to do. You can always count on Him. God never falls out of fashion.

REFLECT

Have you ever seen your favorite celebrity do or say something that was wrong? What was it? Take a moment and write down what would have been the right thing to do in that situation.

_____

_____

_____

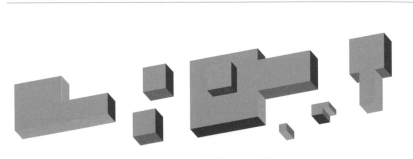

WHOM ARE YOU FOLLOWING?

Finally, brothers and sisters, whatever is true, whatever is noble,
whatever is right, whatever is pure, whatever is lovely,
whatever is admirable—if anything is excellent or
praiseworthy—think about such things.

PHILIPPIANS 4:8

God's Word makes it very clear what kinds of things we should
think about and follow: good news, pure, true, and honest. Basically, stuff that is good for us and shows us the right way. But
sometimes, on social media, you might follow things that don't fit
this description. Because they are funny and popular, or because
they seem cool, you might feel pressure to imitate them—but Jesus
says that you shouldn't.

Jesus wants you to follow His example. To be just, pure, honest,
and loving. The Bible tells us that staying connected with bad
influences corrupts us as well. That means that they can end up
making us worse. We may not think that's going to happen, but it
usually does. The people we see on social media may be funny, but
if they have to be mean or crude or use bad language to do it, you
shouldn't want to be like them.

This can be a hard choice to make. But in the end, you will please
God, and He will be so proud of you for making the honorable
decision. If we follow the example of God's Word instead of negative social media, we will have what's best for us.

REFLECT

Are you on any sites or social media platforms that you feel in your heart just
aren't good for you? If so, write a couple of the sites or platforms down here,
pray, and talk to someone you trust about whom you should unfollow. Then
make the decision that you know is best for you.

_____

_____

_____

YOU ARE MADE TO CREATE

In the beginning God created the heavens and the earth.

GENESIS 1:1

The first thing that we learn about God when we read the Bible is that God is creative. Every animal, tree, mountain, ocean, and part of the earth came from His imagination. Creativity comes naturally to God. When He made the universe and the earth, He made something out of nothing, just like when you or someone you know makes a beautiful drawing out of a blank piece of paper. God loves when you use your imagination to bring out something new. He loves it because it's a reflection of Him. When you create art, make music, write a poem, or have an innovative idea, God is pleased, because you are being just like your Heavenly Father. God made you like Him, so you are made to create just like God.

There is a reason for our creativity—it should point people back to Christ. Your creative works can point people back to Christ by making them feel love, encouragement, hope, and strength as a result of your creation. What you do can inspire others to want to do better themselves. Even if you don't feel like you have artistic talent, you can be creative in designing your room, organizing your closet, creating an app or website, or finding innovative solutions to problems. When you create, you are acting just like your Heavenly Father.

REFLECT

Write down what you think is the most creative thing that God made. What's so creative about it?

_____

_____

_____

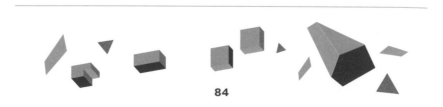

THE RIGHT LINEUP

Walk with the wise and become wise,
for a companion of fools suffers harm.

PROVERBS 13:20

We always enjoy watching sports in our house. It's great to watch your favorite team win—but it can be frustrating to watch them lose. Sometimes, when they are losing, it just doesn't seem like they are playing well together. At that point, it's up to the coach to change the players or switch up the lineup. The coach does this because the right lineup will give the team the best opportunity to get back on track to win.

God is like our head coach. He always wants us to win in life. He knows that the friends you have around you have a lot to do with that. When you have the right people on your team, life is better. Your friends will influence you, and sometimes you will start to become like your friends. If they are nice and make good decisions, you will be nice and make good decisions, too. But if they are mean and act foolishly, you, too, could become mean and foolish. That's why God instructs us to choose friends wisely.

Choose to surround yourself with friends who are good influences, the kind of friends who encourage you to do and say the right things. That is the right lineup that will help you win in life.

REFLECT

What qualities do you like most in a friend? Can you think of a time when you lost a friend but then made a different friend who made you feel better and was a better influence?

_____

_____

_____

FEELING SHY

> Above all, love each other deeply, because love
> covers over a multitude of sins. Offer hospitality to
> one another without grumbling.

1 PETER 4:8–9

Have you ever been called "shy"? You might have thought to yourself, *I'm not shy. I just don't feel like talking to anyone right now.* It's totally okay to want time to yourself to recharge. That is okay, and you deserve that alone time.

You may be feeling a little nervous or timid in the moment, and that's okay, too. When someone is trying to talk to you and thinks you're shy, they actually might be feeling a little insecure themselves. Try giving them a reassuring smile. This will make them feel better, and then both of you might be feeling more comfortable in no time.

When we truly love people like Jesus does, we put the comfort of others before our own. This means, like Jesus, we are hospitable—or warm and welcoming—to others, even when we don't really feel like it. Being polite and kind makes people feel comfortable and accepted. You don't have to carry on a long conversation. But a little eye contact, a smile, and just a few words go a long way. Practicing these three moves will boost your confidence as well.

REFLECT

Do you feel you are shy? Write down why you do or don't think so below, and then discuss it with someone who loves you. If the answer is "yes," ask them to practice the "eye contact, smile, and 'Hello'" move we discussed above. And remember, it's okay to be you!

RESPECTING PERSONAL SPACE

... value others above yourselves, not looking to your own
interests but each of you to the interests of the others.

PHILIPPIANS 2:3B-4

You have the right to be comfortable with the way others touch
you or speak to you. When others respect this, they are honor-
ing you. In addition, you should look out for others by respecting
their privacy and preferences. This is called "consent." Consent
means asking for and getting permission before you do anything
that would impact someone's feelings and respect for privacy
and comfort.

It is really important to get and give consent for things like
touching, and even in-person and internet conversations. In
addition, others should not touch you or speak to you in a way that
you're not comfortable with. If they do, they are not valuing you
properly, and that's not okay.

If you like more personal space and don't want to hug someone,
express how you feel. If someone tries to hug you, try taking a step
back, putting out your hand to them, and saying, "I prefer hand-
shakes instead." You can also ask them not to touch you. It may
feel uncomfortable at first, but if they value you above themselves
(which they should), they will respect your wishes. On the other
hand, if you are a close talker and like a lot of touching, try asking
your friends whether it's okay to stand close to them next time. You
will make them feel valued, and they will really appreciate you for it.

REFLECT

Write down the things you want to express to friends about your personal
space—that you don't like hugging, or that they can always feel free to hug
you, etc.

WHEN OTHERS ARE HURTING

"Which of these three do you think was a neighbor to the man
who fell into the hands of robbers?"
The expert in the law replied, "The one who had mercy on him."

Jesus told him, "Go and do likewise."

LUKE 10:36-37

In one story from the Bible, a man traveling on a road got attacked by two robbers. They beat him up, stole his clothes, and left him half dead. A priest and a temple servant both walked right by and didn't stop to help him. Finally, a Samaritan—a man who normally wouldn't even talk to him—had compassion for him and stopped. He bandaged his wounds, put him on his own donkey, and brought him to a place where he could be taken care of. He even offered to pay the guy's medical bills.

The priest and the temple servant—the two people in this story who you would think would help the hurting man—actually crossed to the other side of the street to avoid him. Have you ever done something like that? When we go out of our way to avoid someone who is hurting, physically or emotionally, we can actually hurt them even more.

Jesus asks us to have compassion on people who are hurting. He asks us to be like the Samaritan: to help others when they are hurting, even if it's a sacrifice for us. When we do this, we are acting like Jesus, and it makes Him so happy.

REFLECT

Is there someone at school who you know might be hurting right now? Write down how you'll be friendly to them, and follow up back here after you do it to write down how it went.

_____

_____

_____

WHEN YOU'RE NOT FEELING LIKE YOURSELF

Hope deferred makes the heart sick,
but a longing fulfilled is a tree of life.

PROVERBS 13:12

Sometimes in life, it seems like everything we hoped for is taken away. When this happens, we feel sad and we may not want to do the things we used to like to do. Sometimes, we just feel sad and alone for a long time and we can't figure out why; it just feels like our heart is "sick." If you feel like this, you should know that you're not alone, and you deserve to feel better. Not only does Jesus want to heal you, but the people whom God has placed in your life love you and want to help, too.

Jesus loves you and can give you hope. When your hope is fulfilled, it gives you life and makes you feel refreshed, joyful, and new. There will be times in life that are low, but you never need to be in a low place for long. You have family and friends who love you. And remember, Jesus loves you and has great things in store for your life. There's always something good coming up around the corner.

REFLECT

If you ever are:

- not feeling like yourself,
- losing interest in things you usually like to do,
- feeling extra sad for long periods of time,
- so stressed that it's making some things in your life harder,

make sure to tell an adult who loves you. If it's hard to talk about your feelings, jot down a little more about your feelings below, and just show this to them.

_____

_____

_____

YOU'RE NOT WEIRD, YOU'RE JUST DIFFERENT

For we are God's handiwork, created in Christ Jesus
to do good works, which God prepared in advance for us to do.

EPHESIANS 2:10

Can you imagine the reactions people had when television was first invented? What about when the first car hit the streets? Or when the internet was introduced? Those creations are all very important to us now, but they might have seemed weird or strange at the time. Sometimes, things are created that are so special, people don't quite know how to receive them.

God created you to be more special than all of those things. He calls you His handiwork. You are one of a kind. You are His very own work of art that He considers a masterpiece. At times, you could be tempted to think that being different is a bad thing. Maybe other kids have called you weird. But being original is the best thing! Your unique ability is what makes this world better.

You are special to God. You are made just the way He wanted you. You are made so perfectly that He stopped making more of you because He perfected the recipe. He didn't want you to be just like everyone else, so He added a little something special to you. Your originality is the special something that makes you *YOU*. And the things that make you special are the things that many people love about you.

REFLECT

What are a few things that you really like about yourself that make you different? Write them down. Then say out loud, "I like this about myself, that I (things that you have written). Thank You, God, for making me so special."

_____

_____

_____

PUTTING OTHERS FIRST

Do nothing out of selfish ambition or vain conceit. Rather, in humility value others above yourselves, not looking to your own interests but each of you to the interests of the others.

PHILIPPIANS 2:3–4

There's an old saying that "a chain is only as strong as its weakest link." That's because even if all the other links are strong, if one weak link breaks, the whole chain will break. Sometimes, this saying is used to talk about teamwork, or community. Your community is made up of the people in the area where you live and the groups that you are connected to, like your church or school. You strengthen this community by being considerate of others, serving others, and putting others first—making sure you are keeping the chain strong.

It's important to God that we value all people, especially those in our community. Because we value them, there will be times when we will have to put their feelings before ours. Putting others first takes humility. Humility is not thinking less of yourself, it's just thinking of yourself less (see the devotion on humility, page 60). Putting others before ourselves is an act of love. And love always makes the chain stronger.

One of the reasons why God put you in your community is to be a blessing to those people. Volunteering your time, energy, and effort to make people feel loved will always better your community.

REFLECT

Think about a time when someone put you first—maybe they helped you while you were playing on a team, or they paid attention to you instead of something else. How did that make you feel?

_____

_____

_____

SHOWING MERCY

Those who are kind benefit themselves,
but the cruel bring ruin on themselves.

PROVERBS 11:17

Have you ever seen a movie where the hero has a chance to destroy the evildoer and instead lets them live? They were showing mercy and giving them a second chance to do right. Mercy is when you show kindness or forgiveness to someone who has done something that normally deserves punishment.

When you're merciful to others, the Bible says that it benefits your mind, heart, and emotions. You feel good about what you've done. You're being the "bigger person." However, when you are cruel or mean (like if that hero had decided to destroy the bad guy while he was begging for mercy), it can make you feel not so great. Have you ever made a bad decision and had a stomachache afterward? It's like that.

God encourages us to show mercy to help others, but also for our own benefit. Not only is that the example that Jesus set for how we are supposed to love others, but it is also really good for our soul and body. Having mercy on others helps you.

REFLECT

Do you have a sibling or family member whom you've been a bit hard on? Write down a way you can show them mercy, and really try to go easy on them this week. Then notice how you feel differently in your mind, emotions, and even physical health. Write your observations here.

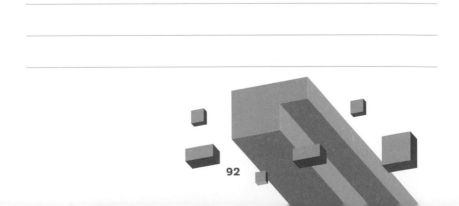

DISCIPLINING YOUR BODY

No discipline seems pleasant at the time, but painful.
Later on, however, it produces a harvest of righteousness
and peace for those who have been trained by it.

HEBREWS 12:11

Sometimes you want to sleep in a little bit later. Or go to bed a little bit later. Sometimes you don't want to brush your teeth or wash your hands. But if you always give in to whatever you feel like in the moment, you will never have any discipline. And when you have no discipline, things in your life start falling apart.

Often, we may not want to do what is best for us. Relaxing on the couch for hours is easier than taking a jog around your neighborhood, but physical discipline teaches us to mentally push past things that are hard. When you discipline yourself, you are training your mind to try hard and fight the feelings of quitting. Discipline makes us more powerful and able to tackle even life's most challenging tasks. It helps us understand that outside forces don't have power over us.

Discipline always comes with rewards. You will learn not to give up. You'll have physical endurance even when you don't feel like continuing. You'll even do better at schoolwork and extracurricular clubs. Discipline is how you become strong—mentally, physically, and emotionally.

REFLECT

Write down some areas in your life where you usually give in to how you feel at the moment. Now write down some ways you can exercise more discipline in these areas.

IN OVER YOUR HEAD

Come to me, all you who are weary and burdened, and I will give you rest. Take my yoke upon you and learn from me, for I am gentle and humble in heart, and you will find rest for your souls.

MATTHEW 11:28–29

For many of us, life can get really busy—you're probably dealing with school assignments, sports practices, family events, and a band recital, all at the same time. It's common to feel overwhelmed when you don't have enough time to get it all done. God knows this, and He has a solution: His rest.

God's rest will help calm the chaos happening in your thoughts and feelings. Rest here doesn't mean taking a nap. It means a calm sense of peace and stillness in your soul. In order to access His rest, we have to come to Him and learn from Him. We have to be open to how God wants to lead us, because He will lead us in the pathways of peace. He does this because He loves us.

One of the ways that God helps you feel less overwhelmed is by bringing order to your day. Ask for God's help, then write out a list of your priorities, with the most important things at the top. Make a schedule for when you'll accomplish each task. Important things should go first. Ask a parent for help to make sure you have done it well. Order will always help you feel less overwhelmed about the day or week.

REFLECT

Remember a time when you have felt overwhelmed. Did it make you feel better when you brought some order to your day or week?

_____

_____

_____

GOD MADE US DIFFERENT

Now you are the body of Christ, and each one of you is a
part of it. The eye cannot say to the hand, "I don't need you!"
And the head cannot say to the feet, "I don't need you!"
But in fact God has placed the parts in the body,
every one of them, just as he wanted them to be.

1 CORINTHIANS 12:27, 21, 18

God has created so many different kinds of people. The Bible says
that together, we are all one body. That means we are all different
parts, just like our body parts. In the body, every part is needed—if
you were made up of all feet, you would probably be pretty stinky,
and you wouldn't be able to see. So we need to have parts that look
very different and have completely different purposes—just like the
world needs all sorts of very different people.

John the Baptist was a really different kind of guy. The Bible says
his clothes were made of camel hair, he ate locusts (big bugs), and
he lived in the wilderness. This was NOT normal for back then. But
he was so important to the body of Christ because he prepared the
way for Jesus to come. He HAD to be unique—even strange—in
order to fulfill his purpose.

There are people you know who are very different, like John the
Baptist. But remember, God made them just as He wanted them to
be, so that they could serve the purpose for which He made them.
Celebrate their differences, knowing that God has a use for them.

REFLECT

Do you know anyone who seems strange or just very different from you?
The Bible says that they are important and that we should treat them well,
with empathy, honor, and dignity. Can you think of anyone you should treat
with more honor?

WHY HOMEWORK IS WORTH IT

All hard work brings a profit, but mere talk leads only to poverty.

PROVERBS 14:23

You may wish that you never had to do homework ever again. When you're doing it, it can seem unnecessary or like a waste of your time. But there's actually a huge benefit to homework. Have you ever played basketball with someone who you know never practices and isn't very good but sure does talk a big game? They are all talk and no hard work. If you've played sports, you know that the only way to get really good at something is to practice until the moves become second nature. That's how the guys in the NBA got there—hard work. And their hard work has brought them a profit.

Homework is just like practice. Your teacher teaches you the material in class, but it may not all stick. You do homework to practice the knowledge you learned at school, so that the information gets deep into your mind and sticks. Then, when it comes time for a test, it's second nature, just like that jump shot.

REFLECT

Write down what you might want to be when you grow up (you can write a few ideas). Then, next to it, list all the subjects in school. Now draw a line from each career to all the different subjects you think might be necessary to prepare for it.

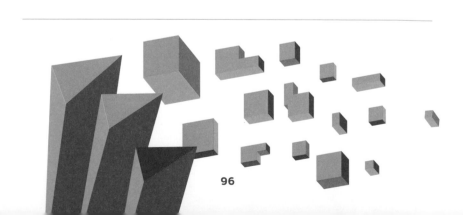

WHAT YOU HAVE IS JUST RIGHT FOR YOU

For where you have envy and selfish ambition,
there you find disorder and every evil practice.

JAMES 3:16

God made you everything you need to be, and He gave you all the gifts and talents you need in order to do what He's called you to do. This is why there is no need to want what anyone else has. You getting what someone else has, or someone else losing what they have, will never make you better. God loves you and has something special planned out *just for you*.

The Bible says that envy is unloving. So whether you wish you had material things, talents, looks, or even friends, being jealous or envious only ends up hurting you and others. God doesn't want you to be jealous of anything your friends have, because it can cause problems, like bad thoughts or even losing your friends. The next time you're tempted to feel envious, remember that who you are is enough, and what you have is just right for you!

REFLECT

Write down five things about yourself that are awesome. The next time you're tempted to feel jealousy or envy toward someone else, take another look at this list.

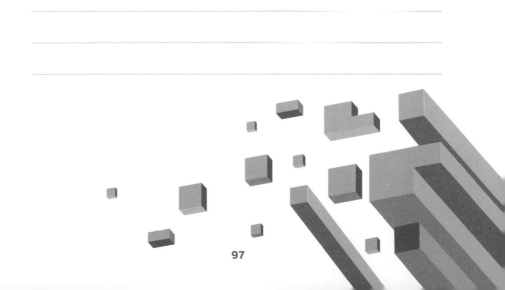

97

TELLING THE TRUTH
DRAWS YOU CLOSER TO GOD

Therefore each of you must put off falsehood and speak
truthfully to your neighbor, for we are all members of one body.

EPHESIANS 4:25

There's an old saying that goes, there are three sides to a story:
his side, her side, and the truth. The truth gets its own category,
because it is *that* important—way more important than anyone's
explanations or complaints. Truth is important to God. In fact, the
Holy Spirit is actually referred to in the Bible as the spirit of truth.
Truth is an expression of God, and God wants us to be imitators of
Him in this way.

It's always right to tell the truth, no matter the situation or who
is around. We can be tempted to lie, especially when there might
be negative consequences for telling the truth (like having your
friends get mad at you). But it's important to tell the truth to our
parents, teachers, siblings, and even our friends. Because God is
a spirit of truth, it's hard to feel close to God when we lie. Lies will
usually lead to more lies and teary eyes, but the truth will lead you
back to God. Good things can happen when you tell the truth, and
it makes you feel free. Most important of all, God wants us to be
loyal to the truth. He loves the truth and He loves us.

If you want to get closer to God, be a young man of truth, for this
is pleasing to God.

REFLECT

Think about the last situation where you could have lied but decided to tell
the truth. Why did you decide to do it? How did telling the truth make you
feel in the days that followed?

_____

_____

_____

SEEING GOOD IN ALL SHAPES AND SIZES

But the LORD said to Samuel, "Do not consider his appearance
or his height, for I have rejected him. The LORD does not
look at the things people look at. People look at the
outward appearance, but the LORD looks at the heart."

1 SAMUEL 16:7

God created people in all different shapes and sizes. You might
be going through a time now where your body is changing, and
things are looking different. Or you might be seeing some of the
other boys growing and changing, and you're wondering when
your changes will come. No matter what shape or size you are, God
loves you just the same. And the most important thing about you is
what's on the inside.

When Samuel came to David's house to choose the next King
of Israel, he came looking for someone who was tall, strong, and
handsome. But God spoke to Samuel and let him know that he was
looking at the wrong thing. It's not what's on the outside but rather
what's on the inside that matters to God. God looks at our hearts.
See, David was small compared to his seven older brothers. However, God still chose him over the other, stronger-looking brothers,
because of his heart.

For God, it's not your height or weight but rather your heart that
determines the kind of person you are.

REFLECT

Ask three friends what they like most about you. Notice that most of the
responses will have nothing to do with your physical appearance. Write
down what they say here, and reread it when you need a pick-me-up.

WHO GOD MADE YOU TO BE

Many are the plans in a person's heart,
but it is the LORD's purpose that prevails.

PROVERBS 19:21

All of us have some idea of what we want to be when we grow up:
a veterinarian, a professional athlete, an architect, a doctor, and a
YouTube star are just a few options. But did you know that God also
has a plan for you? He designed you exactly how He wanted you to
be, so that you would be perfectly suited for the purpose He has for
you. From the color of your hair to the way you think and what you
are good at, God planned all of it, and He wants you to use it for a
great purpose.

You may have plans in your heart to be or do something, but
make sure to ask God what He wants. When you say to your Creator,
"Do what you want with me, Lord," you're telling Him that you trust
Him and His creation. What's awesome about doing what God calls
you to in life is that you end up so much happier and more fulfilled
than when you close your ears to Him and do whatever you feel like
doing. God also knows how you will be happiest. So be sure to seek
God's advice and wisdom about what you are supposed to be, and
trust Him. He has made you for something great!

REFLECT

Take a moment and write a note to the Lord. Say, "Lord, I want to be
_____ when I grow up, but I trust You, and if You want me to
do something else, I'm listening. Please tell me." Then, when you feel like
God has spoken to your heart about your future, write that down as well.

_____

_____

_____

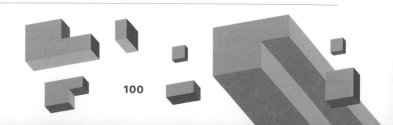

SCRIPTURE INDEX

INDEX OF TOPICS

ABOUT THE AUTHORS

David S. Winston is the pastor of Go Hard for Christ Youth Ministry at Living Word Christian Center and director of Bill Winston Ministries, a worldwide outreach ministry. Both are based in Illinois. He is also the founder of the Winston Leadership Institute. He speaks all over the world, empowering people of all ages to be everything God has called them to be.

Niki Winston serves alongside David overseeing Go Hard for Christ, and together they oversee the LWCC Canaanland Kidz for Christ children's ministry. Niki has written books on marriage and has a passion for teaching how we can love each other better and apply the Word of God in our lives so that it works.

David and Niki live in the Chicagoland area and are blessed to have four wonderful, healthy, happy children: Jacob, Jordan, Joshua, and Lily.